ØDEGAARD

T0019533

MATT AND TOM OLDFIELD

ULTIMATE FOOTBALL HEROES

ØDEGAARD

FROM THE PLAYGROUND
TO THE PITCH

DINO

First published by Dino Books in 2023,
an imprint of Bonnier Books UK,
4th Floor, Victoria House, Bloomsbury Square, London WC1B 4DA
Owned by Bonnier Books,
Sveavägen 56, Stockholm, Sweden

 @UFHbooks
 @footieheroesbks
www.heroesfootball.com
www.bonnierbooks.co.uk

Text © Matt Oldfield 2023
The right of Matt Oldfield to be identified as the author of this work has been
asserted by him in accordance with the Copyright, Designs and Patents Act 1988.

Design by Alessandro Susin

All rights reserved. No part of this publication may be reproduced, stored in a
retrieval system, or transmitted in any form or by any means, without the prior
permission in writing of the publisher, nor be otherwise circulated in any form
of binding or cover other than that in which it is published and without a similar
condition including this condition being imposed on the subsequent purchaser.

Paperback ISBN: 978 1 78946 487 0
E-book ISBN: 978 1 78946 495 5

British Library cataloguing-in-publication data:
A catalogue record for this book is available from the British Library.

Printed and bound in Great Britain by Clays Ltd, Elcograf S.p.A.

3 5 7 9 10 8 6 4 2

All names and trademarks are the property of their respective owners,
which are in no way associated with Dino Books. Use of these
names does not imply any cooperation or endorsement.

For all readers,
young and old(er)

ULTIMATE
FOOTBALL HEROES

Matt Oldfield is a children's author focusing on the wonderful world of football. His other books include *Unbelievable Football* (winner of the 2020 Children's Sports Book of the Year) and the *Johnny Ball: Football Genius* series. In association with his writing, Matt also delivers writing workshops in schools.

Cover illustration by Dan Leydon.
To learn more about Dan visit danleydon.com
To purchase his artwork visit etsy.com/shop/footynews
Or just follow him on Twitter @danleydon

TABLE OF CONTENTS

ACKNOWLEDGEMENTS

First of all I'd like to thank everyone at Bonnier Books for supporting me and for running the ever-expanding UFH ship so smoothly. Writing stories for the next generation of football fans is both an honour and a pleasure. Thanks also to my agent, Nick Walters, for helping to keep my dream job going, year after year.

Next up, an extra big cheer for all the teachers, booksellers and librarians who have championed these books, and, of course, for the readers. The success of this series is truly down to you.

Okay, onto friends and family. I wouldn't be writing this series if it wasn't for my brother Tom. I owe him so much and I'm very grateful for his belief in me as an author. I'm also very grateful to the rest of my family, especially Mel, Noah, Nico, and of course Mum and Dad. To my parents, I owe my biggest passions: football and books. They're a real inspiration for everything I do.

Pang, Will, Mills, Doug, Naomi, John, Charlie, Sam, Katy, Ben, Karen, Ana (and anyone else I forgot) – thanks for all the love and laughs, but sorry, no I won't be getting 'a real job' anytime soon!

And finally, I couldn't have done any of this without Iona's encouragement and understanding. Much love to you, and of course to Arlo, the ultimate hero of all. I hope we get to enjoy these books together one day.

CHAPTER 1

NORTH LONDON DERBY LEGEND

15 January 2023, Tottenham Hotspur Stadium

There's only one Martin Ødegaard!
Martin warmed up with his teammates and dribbled
the ball towards the corner flag, while the Arsenal
fans located in the away end sang his name. When he
waved to them, they sang even louder.

The rest of the crowd had a very different reaction
towards the Arsenal players, and Martin knew that
this was one of the biggest tests of the season so
far – facing fierce rivals Tottenham, who would love
nothing better than to take points from Arsenal after
months of hearing about the Gunners being top

of the table.

Arsenal boss Mikel Arteta had warned his players to be ready for a noisy crowd and some crunching tackles. 'Tottenham will be up for this game,' Mikel said. 'First, we've got to match their energy. If we do that, our talent will give us the edge.'

The build-up to this North London derby had focused on Arsenal's poor away record against Tottenham, but Martin decided to turn that into more motivation.

'In case you didn't know, our last away win against Tottenham was in 2014,' he joked, knowing that his teammates had been hearing and reading about that stat all week. 'Well, it's about time we won then.'

Bukayo Saka was paired with Martin, and they jogged around cones to warm themselves up. 'You like playing against Tottenham,' Bukayo said, reminding Martin that he had scored in this fixture last season. 'Keep making those runs today, and I'll always be looking for you with the cutbacks.'

Back in the dressing room, Martin put on his red-and-white Arsenal shirt and took a deep breath.

Then he pulled the captain's armband into position and stretched his neck from side to side. He still got butterflies in his stomach during these final minutes before walking onto the pitch, and he was always relieved when the players got the knock on the door, the call to go through to the tunnel.

The Tottenham fans roared a big welcome to their own players, and Martin knew that every Arsenal touch would be met with boos early in the game. But part of his job as captain was to settle everyone down and get control of the game in midfield.

An early pass over the top put Bukayo through on the right wing, and Martin sprinted to catch up with his teammate. But Bukayo didn't need him this time; he created an angle for a cross and hammered the ball towards the near post. It caught the Tottenham keeper by surprise, and he fumbled it into his own net.

The stadium went silent, and Martin ran over to Bukayo. Both pretended to take a basketball shot for his goal celebration.

That first goal knocked Tottenham off balance. Some teams might have been happy to sit back and protect the lead, but this Arsenal squad was different – and Martin urged his teammates to keep flying around and winning tackles.

Bukayo was causing problems again on the right wing and, as extra defenders shifted over towards him, he clipped a pass back inside to Martin. He had room to take a few strides forward and then struck a low shot that was heading for the net until the keeper pushed it away.

Martin had an almost identical chance a few minutes later. Again, he hit it hard and low with his left foot, but this time the placement was even better. The shot skidded off the pitch and arrowed into the bottom corner. *2–0!*

Goooooooooooooooooooooaaaaaaaaaaaaaaaaallllllllllllll lllllllllllll!!!!!!!!!!!!!!!!!!!!

'You just can't give Martin Ødegaard that kind of space,' Bukayo said in his best commentator voice as they jogged back to the halfway line. 'Seriously, though, it's like they've never seen you shoot before!'

Arsenal were on the way to another important win and still proving the doubters wrong. While some people were expecting the Gunners to slip up, there was no sign of them stumbling so far. There was still a long way to go in the title race, but Martin was so proud of how the team was playing.

As he joined his teammates to applaud the Arsenal fans before heading back to the dressing room, Martin couldn't stop smiling. Still only twenty-four, his football career had been a wild ride, bursting onto the scene as a teenager, and then battling to maintain his early promise. At Arsenal, though, he finally felt at home.

CHAPTER 2

DAD'S BIGGEST FAN

With the smell of chips and sausages in the air, Martin's eyes were darting around in all directions to make sure he didn't miss anything. He was only five, but he had been counting the days until this special treat ever since he first heard about it.

He followed his mum, Lene, and older brother, Kristoffer, as they weaved through a big group of men and women who all had blue-and-white scarves.

Then Martin saw it. A flash of green between two signs. The Sandefjord pitch! Martin's dad, Hans Erik, played for Sandefjord, and today was the first time that Martin would see him in action.

'Come on, Martin,' Kristoffer called. 'This way!'

Martin snapped out of his daydream. He suddenly realised that he was just standing still and blocking the way; two fans had to swerve at the last second to avoid bumping into him.

He ran to catch up and they all turned the corner together. A tall man with a friendly face waved to them from the end of the corridor. He welcomed Lene and patted Kristoffer on the shoulder, before turning to Martin and passing him a team sheet. Martin recognised the Sandefjord badge on his jacket.

'You must be Martin,' the man said, smiling and shaking his hand. 'Ready to get a closer look at the pitch?'

'Yes!' Martin said instantly, hopping from one foot to the other in excitement.

They followed the tall man through a side door which opened onto a path down to the greenest of green pitches. 'Wow!' was all Martin could say. His eyes were wide with amazement. He could see the dugout, the scoreboard and a few of the players warming up.

'Perfect timing!' a voice called suddenly from behind

Martin's shoulder.

They all turned to see Hans Erik jogging over to them in his warm-up kit. He ducked under a barrier and climbed through to the bottom of the stand, next to the front row of seats.

'What do you think?' he asked Martin, putting his arm round him.

'So cool!' Martin replied. 'I can't wait for the game to start.'

Hans Erik smiled. 'Good! Well, I just wanted to say hi. I've got to get ready, but I'll see you later on. Remember to cheer extra loud for us!'

'Good luck!' Martin and Kristoffer called, as Hans Erik hugged Lene and then rejoined his teammates on the pitch.

The tall man reappeared with good news. 'We've got some VIP seats for you,' he said, looking very proud. 'Follow me.'

He led the way to three seats right on the halfway line, with a perfect view of all the action. Martin was small enough that he could stand up without blocking anyone's view. That was a relief – because he was

bouncing out of his seat before the game had
even started.

'The pitch looks big enough for a hundred players!'
he called out, pulling on his brother's sleeve repeatedly
to get his attention. 'The goals are huge too! How are
the goalkeepers expected to save any shots?'

Lene laughed. 'Kristoffer, you were just like this at
your first game too!'

A few minutes later, Kristoffer nudged Martin and
pointed across to the far side of the stadium where
the teams were coming onto the pitch. Martin jumped
out of his seat, trying to get a closer look. He cheered
loudly as he caught sight of his dad.

The stadium was filling up and there was blue and
white everywhere. It seemed like the whole town was
there to watch the game – and his dad was playing in it!

Once the game started, Martin's eyes rarely left the
pitch. A spaceship could have landed nearby, and he
wouldn't have noticed. Occasionally, he watched the
faces of the fans too – the excitement at kick-off, the
joy when Sandefjord raced forward and the nerves
when the away team was attacking.

Martin didn't know the words to sing the songs, but he clapped and joined in with the chants of 'Sandefjord! Sandefjord!' The whole afternoon was like a dream.

Suddenly, there was an 'Ooooooh' from the crowd and Martin was out of his seat again. He saw a Sandefjord striker running towards the goal ahead of two defenders.

'Go on! Go on!' Martin whispered to himself as he felt his heart beating faster.

The striker took one more touch and then fired a low shot. Martin watched, as if in slow motion, as the ball rolled towards the net. The goalkeeper dived but he couldn't reach it. The ball bounced off the inside of the post and over the line.

Goooooooooooooooooooaaaaaaaaaaaaaaaaallllllllllllll llllllllllll!!!!!!!!!!!!!!!!!!

Sandefjord had scored! The roar from the crowd was one of the loudest noises that Martin had ever heard. He jumped up and down, hugging Kristoffer and his mum.

Martin cheered even louder when his dad had the

ball in midfield. Hans Erik seemed to be everywhere at once – sprinting forward, sprinting back, passing, winning tackles and heading the ball. By the end of the game, Martin's voice was croaky from all his shouting and he felt like he had been playing a full match himself. But it was worth it. Sandefjord had won!

'You're a lucky charm!' Lene said as they left the stadium and walked with the other fans.

'Well, I guess that means I'll have to come to every game,' Martin replied, grinning.

CHAPTER 3

NEW PITCH, NEW POSSIBILITIES

Martin winced as his mum cleaned up a cut on his right elbow. Every time it seemed to be healing, he would fall again playing football and make it worse. Part of the problem was Drammen's gravel pitch. Though it was local and usually had space for Martin to play, it was painful every time he fell.

Even so, that pitch was the first place that Martin wanted to go after school and at weekends. Sometimes he would tag along with Kristoffer and try to keep up with the older kids; at other times he went with a group of his own friends from their school just up the street. Everyone lived nearby, so plans came together easily.

As with Martin, many of the other kids would get injured whenever they fell on the hard surface, and it was a nightmare when the games were played so competitively. No one wanted to lose, and it was often almost dark before their parents finally managed to get them home.

When Hans Erik and Lene met up with their neighbours at a local Drammen festival, it didn't take long for the conversation to drift to the subject of football. The parents all agreed that there had to be a better way for their kids to play the sport they loved – and it gave Hans Erik an idea.

'What if we replace the gravel pitch with a new grass pitch?' he asked.

At first, the other parents weren't sure if he was joking. Some of them laughed. 'Have you had a magic wand all this time without telling us, Hans Erik?' one man replied.

But a few voices clearly liked the idea and were interested in how it might work.

'That would make such a difference,' one woman said. 'With the way the kids race around, they need a safer place to play. We're lucky that there haven't been any serious injuries yet.'

'If we split the costs and get enough people to chip in, we could actually do this,' an older man added.

Still, it wouldn't be cheap. Hans Erik started to make some calls, finding companies that could remove the old pitch and set up the new one. Other parents began to spread the word about a new grass pitch in Drammen, looking for people willing to help with the costs.

After more conversations and meetings, Hans Erik came home one evening with a big envelope under his arm.

'It's happening!' he called. 'Drammen is getting a new grass football pitch!'

Martin, Kristoffer and their sisters, Emilie and Mari, hurried down the stairs, screaming in celebration.

'Can we go and see it?' little Mari asked.

Hans Erik and Lene laughed, wrapping her in a hug. 'Well, it's not ready yet,' Hans Erik said. 'These things take time to build. But you won't have to wait long.'

Martin watched eagerly as the workers arrived to

clear the gravel and started measuring for the grass. But a few days before the new pitch was unveiled, his parents made him promise not to peek at the progress. 'We want it to be a surprise!' his mum insisted.

When the pitch was finally ready, the family walked over together. Martin tucked a football under his arm and tried to control his excitement. As they turned the corner, a big green pitch was right in front of them, with big nets at both ends.

'This is… just… wow!' Martin said, looking in shock at the pitch and then back at his parents. 'I've got to try it out.'

He raced off, dribbling the ball and feeling the grass under his feet. 'No more cuts and bruises!' he called, throwing himself on the floor and rolling around. 'I feel like a real footballer on this pitch!'

His parents laughed. Hans Erik jogged over and stood in goal, daring Martin to take a shot. 'Alright, let's have it then,' he said, grinning. 'Give me your hardest shot.'

Martin didn't need to be told twice. He ran forward, tapping the ball from one foot to the other. Then he stopped, pretending to be unsure of what to do next. It worked. His dad looked confused and started to ask a question. Martin took his chance and quickly sprung back to life, firing a shot towards the bottom corner.

Hans Erik saw he had been tricked and tried to recover. But it was too late. The ball crossed the line before he could get a foot on it.

Goooooooooooooooooooooaaaaaaaaaaaaaaaaaalllllllllllllll lllllllllllll!!!!!!!!!!!!!!!!!!!!

'You little rascal!' Hans Erik laughed, scooping the ball out of the net.

But Martin could barely hear his dad. He was too busy running round the pitch with his T-shirt pulled up over his face, arms in the air, celebrating like he had scored the winning goal in the World Cup final.

Lene smiled as she walked across the grass, admiring how good it looked. 'I have a feeling we're going to be spending a lot of time here!' she said, and gathered the family together near the centre circle for the first of many photos on Drammen's new pitch.

CHAPTER 4

DRAMMEN STRONG

While Martin's footballing career was just beginning, Hans Erik's playing days were nearing an end. He was still getting used to that decision and considering his options on what to do next. No one was shy about giving Hans Erik suggestions either. After hundreds of conversations, the list was still long, but the most popular idea was clear: football coaching.

On a sunny late afternoon walk around the local neighbourhood, he saw lots of children – often the same age as Martin – kicking a ball around in the garden or on the Drammen pitch.

When his dad arrived home, Martin could see a new look on his face. Something had changed during his walk. Sure enough, Hans Erik had made a decision. He would create a new Drammen youth football team and coach the young players.

'This feels right,' he said to the rest of the Ødegaard family around the dining room table. 'It's such an exciting challenge and there are so many talented footballers in this area.'

And one of those promising players was sitting right opposite Hans Erik. 'Please, please, please!' Martin begged. 'I really want to play for this team.'

'As long as the coach sees that you're finishing your homework, I'm sure he'll consider it,' Lene said, winking at her husband.

'I knew you were going to say that!' Martin replied, laughing. 'I'll work extra hard at school, I promise.'

'Okay then,' Hans Erik said. 'Welcome to the team!'

There was a lot more planning to do, and soon Hans Erik had found a club to partner with on his new project. 'You know the Drammen Strong sports club? We're going to be their new youth football team,' he announced proudly later that week.

'Drammen Strong,' Martin repeated. 'I like it!'

As he slotted his shin pads under his socks and put on his trainers, Martin really wasn't sure what to expect. They were training at the Drammen pitch that he knew so well, but everything else felt different. He always enjoyed playing football there with his friends, but that wasn't a real league. There were no referees or coaches. Some days, there were four kids; other days, there were twenty-four.

Drammen Strong quickly felt like a real team. They had a kit, they had proper nets and sometimes they even had fans too! Hans Erik had been busy for weeks, arranging matches against other local youth teams and planning fun training sessions. Martin had never seen his dad with so much energy.

At the first team practice, Martin recognised a few faces from his school and others who often joined in at weekends. He tried to learn all their names so he could call for the ball, and it didn't take long for him to shine as Drammen Strong's brightest young star.

Hans Erik split the kids into small groups, arranged each group in a circle and then picked two boys to start in the middle.

'Right, these two are our chasers,' he said, pointing to the boys putting on orange bibs over their T-shirts. 'The rest of you have to pass the ball around the circle without them intercepting it. If they get to the ball first, the person who played the pass replaces them in the middle.'

Martin bounced on the spot, getting ready for the ball to come his way. When it did, he avoided the chasers with a quick pass to his left. When the ball looped back to him, he dummied to hit the same kind of pass again, then flicked it to his right instead.

'Next, get into pairs,' Hans Erik shouted, after blowing his whistle. 'We're going to do some quick 2 vs 2 drills on the small pitch here. First goal wins, and then you all go to the back of the line.'

Martin paired up with a boy called Alex from his school. In their first 'battle', Martin got the ball with space to take a touch. He ran forward and got away from his marker with a quick change of direction. Now the other defender appeared, and Martin crossed the ball to set up a tap-in for Alex.

In their next time on the pitch, Martin chose to

go it alone. He knocked the ball past a defender, who wasn't expecting that at all, and easily got to it first. Then he took a quick shot from an almost impossible angle and grinned as the ball arrowed into the net.

During each training session, Hans Erik worked hard to nurture the boys' confidence with their first touch and their passing – but in games, the strategy often turned into 'get the ball to Martin'. That plan was usually unstoppable. Martin had such good ball control, and he was so fast when he set off on a run. As defenders tried to keep up, he weaved in and out, spinning them around until they were stumbling and falling.

'Great run!' his dad called out, passing Martin his water bottle. 'Just make sure you keep your head up so you can always find your teammates.'

Hans Erik noticed something else about his son in these early weeks of the Drammen Strong experiment: he hated to lose. As Martin chased back and urged his teammates to keep running, Hans Erik could only look at the ground and laugh to himself. Like father, like son – Martin just loved to compete.

When Drammen Strong kicked off their mini league season with their first game, Martin was dressed in his kit at the front door an hour early. It had taken him a long time to fall asleep the night before, and he couldn't wait to be running all over the pitch.

That morning turned out to be even better than he imagined. Martin scored five goals, Drammen Strong won 7–1 and Hans Erik couldn't stop smiling – a combination of pride about Martin's magical performance and happiness about his first win as a coach.

At breakfast the next morning, Emilie walked into the kitchen and stopped next to Martin. 'Why is there a sheet of paper on your bedroom door with a number six?' she asked.

'It's my countdown,' he answered, taking another sip of his orange juice.

Lene and Hans Erik looked round with confused faces. 'A countdown to what?' Lene said.

'Six days until our next game,' Martin replied, as if it was the most obvious answer in the world.

'Ah yes, of course,' Lene said, grinning and turning

to Hans Erik. 'To be honest, Martin, I'm surprised your dad hasn't put one on our door too!'

They all burst into laughter as Hans Erik took some paper from the kitchen counter, drew a big '6' on it and went upstairs.

CHAPTER 5

ARSENAL FIFA MAGIC

As the clouds got darker and darker on a winter morning, the rain poured down. Martin had been supposed to meet his friends over at the pitch, but those plans were off. For once, he knew he would have to find something else to do. There would be no football on the Drammen pitch today.

He sat down in a chair by the window and pictured himself dribbling through the rain, scoring goals and sliding on his knees to celebrate in the puddles. Then he pictured his parents' reactions if he came home with wet, muddy clothes… hmmm, probably not the best idea.

His brother joined him at the table with a bowl of

cereal, looking outside as the rain rattled on the roof.

'So, no football today, I guess,' Kristoffer said, a disappointed look on his face.

Martin shook his head, looking just as sad, and took a sip of his water. 'Maybe tomorrow.'

'Want to play FIFA?' Kristoffer asked. 'If we can't play football ourselves, this is the next best thing.'

That got Martin's attention.

'You're on!' He jumped up and hurried over to the sofa, picking up the two video game controllers and setting up the TV.

'I'm playing as Barcelona,' Kristoffer said. 'Who do you want?'

Martin paused for a minute. Usually, he would have picked Real Madrid or Ajax or Bayern Munich. But today called for something different.

'I'm going to play as an English team,' he said. 'Just give me whichever team comes up first. I'm feeling that confident!'

'Okay,' Kristoffer said, with a grin. 'You've got Arsenal. That's pretty good.'

The game loaded, and Martin saw the Arsenal crest

and their red-and-white shirt. Those were two of the colours from the Norway team shirt too, and that had to be a good sign.

'Alright, let's do this, Arsenal,' he said quietly when the game-version of the players came onto the screen. 'Oh Thierry Henry, I know him.'

He soon knew lots of the other players' names too – Cesc Fàbregas, Robin van Persie, Robert Pires, Freddie Ljungberg, Sol Campbell.

'That's it. Campbell,' Martin mumbled to himself. 'Pass it forward.' Sometimes he was so focused on the game that he forgot he wasn't actually on the pitch himself.

After three quick passes in midfield, Martin tapped away on his controller and scored with a Fàbregas long shot. Again and again, he used Pires and van Persie to dribble forward, and Henry was always there to sprint through and shoot. 'Henry is too fast for Puyol!' he sang, while Kristoffer was shaking his head.

With more skilful moves, Martin raced into a 3–0 lead. 'Whoa, this is my kind of team,' he said, struggling to believe how easily he was scoring.

'The players are so fast! Even the defenders have skills.'

Martin's wins were rare against his brother, and Kristoffer looked at him in shock. 'Have you been practising secretly?' he asked suspiciously.

'Today's just my day,' Martin replied, winking.

The game finished 5–1 and both brothers sat in silence for a few seconds.

'Well played, bro,' Kristoffer eventually said, high-fiving him. 'But I want a rematch! I'm switching to Juventus for this one.'

'I'm sticking with Arsenal,' Martin said. 'How could I change after that performance? I love this team.'

There were a few local places to watch Premier League games on TV, and Martin usually liked to watch Liverpool play. But he reminded himself to ask his dad when Arsenal were playing next. He wanted to keep an eye on them.

The rematch was much closer, but Thierry Henry was Martin's not-so-secret weapon. With the score locked at 2–2 in the final seconds, he sent Henry on another dribbling run for the game-winning goal. He raised his controller in the air and did his silliest celebration.

They both started laughing, and Martin ducked to dodge the cushion that Kristoffer threw playfully across the sofa.

'Watch out, Arsène Wenger!' Kristoffer said loudly. 'There's a new Arsenal boss in town!'

Martin laughed again. 'I'll admit that I didn't know much about Arsenal before this morning, but I'm a big fan now,' he said.

CHAPTER 6

TRAINING LIKE THE PROS

While Martin grew bigger and stronger, football was never far from his thoughts. He was the star of the Drammen Strong team and scouts from Norway's top clubs were starting to pay close attention. But he didn't want to waste any time, and he knew he could improve even faster with a bit more help.

There were lots of other boys his age at school who loved football and really wanted to become professional footballers when they were older. But Martin had a secret weapon – his dad.

Hans Erik had a front row seat to watch Martin playing for Drammen Strong every week, and he could see his son's huge talent developing. It wasn't just the goals that Martin could score, it was the way he moved to create space and the happiness he seemed to get from setting up his teammates.

Still, Hans Erik didn't want to rush things. Martin was still only eight, and he was enjoying his football. That was the most important thing at his age. But it didn't take long for Martin to show how serious he was about becoming a better player.

'Dad, can we do some training like the pros?' Martin asked one morning. 'Can you show me some of the drills you did at Strømsgodset or Sandefjord?'

Those two little questions kicked off a detailed training plan. 'If you're sure this is what you want, let's really go for it,' Hans Erik said, setting up cones on the Drammen pitch and explaining what he wanted Martin to do.

They started with some of the usual drills from the Drammen Strong training sessions – and when Martin completed them easily, Hans Erik started adding harder parts to really test him.

'Here's another one we used to do,' Hans Erik explained. 'Stand in front of the orange cone. You've got a red cone to your left and a red cone to your right. I'm going to throw the ball to you, and I want you to give me a side-foot layoff, then run round one of the red cones and come back to the orange cone for another layoff. We're going to do this ten times, as fast as you can.'

Martin nodded, jumping up and down on the spot ready to get started. He watched the ball carefully, cushioned a side-foot volley back to his dad, then sprinted around the red cone on his left. After ten layoffs, he was out of breath. They took a quick break, then he jogged over to the orange cone again. 'Let's do ten more,' he said, as Hans Erik got back into position.

When the weather got worse, they moved inside to the local indoor sports hall – and Martin threw himself into all the drills with his usual energy.

At first, Martin just followed every word his dad said about each exercise, but soon he was suggesting his own creative ideas on how to work on his control, passing, shooting, and more. Any equipment in the sports hall usually ended up being used in their workout sessions, from benches and chairs to skipping ropes and beanbags.

Hans Erik welcomed the ideas and turned them into drills focused on decision-making and vision. 'It's one thing to work on accurate passes and take shots against a keeper, but those drills don't always help with awareness on the pitch.'

'What do you mean?' Martin asked, looking a little confused.

Hans Erik dribbled a ball into the middle of the sports hall. 'Wherever you are on the pitch, you should always have a clear picture of where everyone else is – your marker, your nearest teammate, his marker, your strikers and the runs they're making,' he said, glancing in all directions to explain the point to Martin. 'The good players can process that information once the ball comes to them, but the great players have that picture ready before the ball even arrives.'

'But what if I'm so busy keeping an eye on all that stuff and then I'm not ready for the pass when it comes to me?'

'You'll get used to it,' Hans Erik replied, jogging over to get a ball. 'If I pass the ball to you now as if we're in a game and I don't tell you anything, you'll have no idea of whether you have time to take a touch, whether you need to change direction, or where your simplest pass is.'

Martin nodded. 'I'd have to work out all of that while dribbling with the ball.'

'So that's the difference. If you've processed some of the information already, you get a head-start. You'll still need to take those little glances over your shoulder to make sure the picture hasn't changed, but this is where the top players use their brains as well as their feet.'

Martin grinned. He loved getting this special advice, and he was pretty sure that he wouldn't have learned anything like that on the playground with his friends.

'Okay, time to practise it,' Hans Erik said, setting up more cones. 'Each of these cones is a defender. Take a second to see where they are and then I want you to control the pass in a way that gives you the most space.' He paused, then passed the ball to Martin. 'Okay, go!'

Martin had spotted that there were two cones

behind him and another two just to his right. So he controlled the ball, cushioning it to his left and then dribbling forward a few steps.

'Well done!' Hans Erik called out, clapping and then moving some of the cones to change the picture and keep Martin off balance. 'Let's do it again. Remember, trust yourself to make quick decisions.'

Martin gulped down some water and passed the ball back. He would stay here all day if his dad let him.

After months of working together early in the morning and after school, Martin really understood what it meant to 'see the game' – and Hans Erik knew the time had come for his son to move on to the next level.

'I love our time together and we'll keep doing this, but you're ready for bigger challenges too,' he said, putting an arm round Martin's shoulders. 'I think it's time to speak to Strømsgodset about a trial for their youth team.'

CHAPTER 7

STRØMSGODSET AND THE ELITE ACADEMY

The trial at Strømsgodset lasted under twenty minutes. Once the coaches saw what Martin could do with the ball at his feet, they began hurriedly preparing the paperwork before another club could swoop in.

'You just don't see that kind of talent at the Under 11 level,' Harald Johannessen, one of the main coaches, said, shaking his head in amazement. 'In fact, his skills are already so advanced that we may need to put him in an older age group.'

There were sighs of relief from everyone at Strømsgodset when Martin made it official and joined the youth team. He was quickly moved up to play against the older boys.

'What position do you play?' Harald asked Martin at the next session while they waited for the other boys to arrive.

For some reason, that wasn't a question Martin had expected. Was 'everywhere' an acceptable answer? No, probably not, he thought. 'Anywhere in midfield,' he finally replied. 'But mostly right wing.'

Harald nodded. 'I could see last week that you love to cut inside from the right onto your left foot,' he said. 'You seemed to create a goal every time you did it.'

Though Martin was one of the quietest in the youth team, he became good friends with the other players. Of course, winning games together always helped with those friendships – and Strømsgodset had been doing a lot of that lately. Week after week, Martin had a new skill to try out in training and there were usually shrieks of laughter if he managed to trick one of the defenders.

In his own way, he became a leader too. Even when he was dominating games and practice sessions, there was no ego in the way he acted, and he encouraged his teammates whenever they made a mistake or were having a bad game.

When Martin turned eleven, more opportunities emerged. He was invited to the Elite Academy, an even higher level for the best players in local teams and met another group of boys who loved football just as much as he did.

'This is going to be a step up, but you're ready,' Harald told him. 'You'll be able to build on the work we've been doing and test yourself against really good defenders. I've already told the other coaches what a special player you are.'

But Martin wasn't going to be training with other eleven-year-olds at the Elite Academy. Again, he was promoted to work with the older boys, which gave him the chance to progress even faster. At first, he was added to the Under 13s. Martin was used to being the youngest and smallest player on the pitch from his games with Kristoffer's friends, and he had shown that he could handle it.

Martin could see why the coaches wanted to test him, though. It was good for him to deal with tough tackles and get used to more physical defending. He was pushed off the ball sometimes – but only when the defenders could catch him! Through it all, he was fearless with the ball, playing with his usual freedom and trying all kinds of tricks. Before long, he was on the radar of the Under 16 coaches too.

One of the main things Martin noticed at the Elite Academy was how he could adjust his game with so many good players around him. In the past, he had been trying to do everything – running back, running forward, tackling, taking throw-ins, taking free kicks, trying to dribble round the whole defence.

But he soon realised that he didn't need to do all of that at the Elite Academy. He could save some energy and just focus on what he did best.

With the Under 13s, Martin started at left-back. 'Don't worry,' one of the coaches said, sensing Martin's uncertainty. 'We know you love to attack, and you'll still get to do lots of that. But this should protect you from some of the bumps and bruises, and you'll be really dangerous with your pace and crossing.'

That sounded good to Martin. He never thought

he would be trusted as a defender, but he quickly saw that his coaches were right. No wingers were fast enough to get away from him, and then he was a nightmare for the opposition when he raced forward to support the attack. He piled up assists with crosses and through balls for the team's strikers, and he still got to play some minutes as a winger.

Even among other highly rated players, Martin had the 'wow' factor in everything he did. Whether it was his perfectly placed free kicks, his effortless no-look passes or his dribbling runs that left defenders on the ground, he was the Elite Academy star who shone the brightest – and the one who most of the scouts were showing up to see.

CHAPTER 8

YOUNG MESSI

Somehow being 'the next big thing' could be both exciting and terrifying at the same time. Martin's life was changing quickly as he passed every new football test, with the expectations growing bigger and bigger. One week, people were calling him a future Norway star, then he was going to be a European star, then a global star.

Some days, Martin couldn't help but smile about it all. Mostly, though, he just wanted to block out all that talk and focus on playing football. Everyone wanted to compare him with other players and try to predict what would happen next, but he wasn't even a teenager yet.

'Here's Young Messi!' one of his Strømsgodset teammates called out, high-fiving Martin as they got ready for training.

'Young Messi' was the latest nickname that had started to appear on TV shows, in tweets and apparently now within the Strømsgodset team too.

That comparison felt especially strange to Martin. In his bedroom, he had Messi posters on two of the walls, and the Barcelona superstar had become his favourite player. There was nothing that Messi couldn't do. Martin tried to think like Messi when he was running with the ball, but big pressure came with comparisons to an all-time great player.

Martin's usual response was to brush it off. 'Stop it, there's only one Messi!' he liked to say.

But scouts recognised some of the same qualities. Like Messi, Martin was left-footed, they both liked to cut in from the right wing, could create space so easily with quick feet and clever movement, and both looked skinny as they darted around the pitch. All reports pointed to Martin as the type of player who only comes along once every ten years.

If it was even possible, Martin's reputation jumped to a higher level after some mind-blowing performances at one of Norway's Under 16 tournaments. Martin was only twelve, playing against the country's best fifteen-year-olds, but he was the one that everyone was talking about.

'He just sees the game differently,' one of the scouts whispered on the phone. 'He's got all the skills and he understands when to use them. He could be one of the best players in the world in five years.' Coaches and scouts were being even more secretive now, knowing that they might all be competing for Martin's signature at some point.

When Martin returned from the tournament, he got a warm welcome from the Strømsgodset youth team coaches – and some exciting news. For some time, the coaches had been discussing possible next steps for Martin and now it felt like there was only one decision that made sense, even if it was a wild one.

'We've loved having you with us in the youth teams,' Harald said, with some sadness in his voice. 'Honestly, these have been some of my favourite years as a coach. But our top priority has always been helping you get the most out of your talent – and that means moving you on to the first team.'

'Wait, what?!' Martin said, staring and looking around the room at the other coaches. 'But… I'm thirteen. Is that even allowed?'

Harald laughed. 'It's a fair question but yes, we've checked and you're all set to join the training sessions,' he said. 'You've earned this opportunity with your hard work and we're all going to be cheering you on.'

'There are so many great guys in the first team too,' another coach added. 'They'll take good care of you.'

Martin smiled, suddenly feeling an odd mixture of happiness and sadness. He would really miss his youth team coaches and his teammates but playing for the Strømsgodset first team was something he had dreamed about.

'I'll always remember everything you've done for me,' he said, hugging each of the coaches, then getting his phone out of his pocket to share the news with his family. 'I guess I've got some phone calls to make.'

CHAPTER 9

A BIG FIRST IMPRESSION IN THE FIRST TEAM

When Martin arrived for his first training session with the Strømsgodset first team, there was something comforting about having his dad with him – and not just as his driver. Hans Erik was now an assistant coach with Strømsgodset.

'Remember, I'll be there, so you're not going through this alone,' Hans Erik said as they drove into the car park next to the training field. 'You should be so proud of yourself. This is an incredible step, so just enjoy it.'

Martin nodded. He had been quiet for most of the journey, juggling a mix of emotions. He was excited but nervous: eager to learn but shy about talking to so many new people. He picked up his bag from the back seat, took a deep breath and followed his dad towards the pitch.

Martin had wondered many times about what kind of reaction he would get from the other first team players.

'I'm sure they'll mainly be curious,' Lene had suggested, giving him a supportive hug. 'There's been so much talk about you around the club already, and they'll have heard the stories from your games with the youth teams.'

Martin looked ahead and saw a few players starting to warm up at the far end. He hoped his mum was right.

It helped that he had spent time around Strømsgodset, with the Under 13s and the Under 16s. Just as the first team players probably knew who he was, Martin was confident that he would recognise most of them.

Hans Erik pointed the way to the first team dressing room – they had agreed that it would look better for Martin to introduce himself rather than relying on his dad to do it. He pushed the dressing room door open and stepped inside.

Before he even saw any of the other players, he smelt the smells that he knew well from being around his dad's playing days – the mix of sweat, muscle spray and deodorant.

Then conversations stopped as the players turned to see who had walked in. Martin paused and urged himself not to freeze. 'Hi,' he mumbled.

Thankfully, the Strømsgodset players sensed that this might be a difficult moment for a thirteen-year-old kid. The two men nearest to him hurried over to shake his hand. 'Welcome, Martin!' one of them said. 'I'm Marius and this is Péter. This is a big day for you!'

'Looking forward to having you with us in training,' Péter added. 'We know they wouldn't have promoted you if you weren't a really talented player.'

'Just go easy on us old guys!' called another new teammate, who looked easily old enough to be Martin's father.

Martin laughed.

'Is there somewhere I should sit?' he asked, not

wanting to take someone's favourite spot.

'Anywhere you want,' Péter Kovács replied. 'But I think they've put your training kit over there.' He pointed to the bench opposite.

On the pitch, Martin began to feel the nerves disappear. It was easier to do his talking with a ball at his feet. From talking to his dad, he knew that the fastest way to earn the other players' respect wasn't to show off his skills or try to score spectacular goals – it was by proving he could handle the hard work of being a professional footballer.

So he kept his head down and did exactly what the coaches told him. He kept pace with the fastest runners as they jogged five laps of the pitch, he did all the warm-up stretches more carefully than he had ever done before, and he didn't say much to anyone.

Martin had been so worried about meeting the other players that he had forgotten he was now playing with, and against, grown men. They were bigger and stronger than he was, and they knew all the tricks to shield the ball.

When the proper drills started, Martin was thankful

that his dad had shown him so many of them over the years. Nothing seemed too scary, and he had chances to show he was a good dribbler and passer.

In one of the drills, a Strømsgodset defender bumped into Martin as they went for a loose ball. Martin just bounced off him. He managed to stay on his feet but only after a few wobbling steps. It was a good reminder that he would need to get stronger to survive in the first team against grown men.

The session opened up even more for Martin when the 3 vs 3 mini games started. This was his first real chance to demonstrate his skills and his speed. He was put on the green team with Péter and Marius Høibråten. 'Good, let the other defenders look silly when a thirteen-year-old is running circles around them,' Marius said, looking a little relieved.

The pitch was small for 3 vs 3, but Martin knew how to make the most out of the space. Even though he hadn't played with Marius and Péter before, he watched their movement and quickly understood how to make sure he wasn't getting in their way by running into the same areas.

When the other team gave the ball away, Martin sprinted forward on the right. Marius poked a pass towards him, but Martin already had a plan before the ball arrived. A defender rushed across, and Martin took a quick touch inside. The defender was completely wrong-footed and slipped as he tried to change direction.

With a couple of stepovers, Martin glided past another tackle and rolled a shot into the little net.

Goooooooooooooooooooooaaaaaaaaaaaaaaaaallllllllllllll llllllllllll!!!!!!!!!!!!!!!!!!!!

'Woah!' one coach said, more loudly than he meant to, as Strømsgodset manager Ronny Deila joined him by the side of the pitch. 'That boy is so fast he turns defenders into statues.'

'I'll just say this: I'm glad you're on our team!' Marius said, sending everyone into fits of laughter.

Martin felt more freedom to play his attacking style in each training session. Rather than thinking he was a show-off, his teammates told him to keep bringing out the skills and taking risks with the ball – and he was learning a lot from them about how to train, how to

eat the right food and how to deal with wins
and losses.

During the season, Strømsgodset had arranged a
few friendlies to keep the squad fresh and work on
new tactics. When the coaches announced the team
for the upcoming game against Mjøndalen, Martin was
shocked and delighted to be named as one of the subs.

'You really deserve this,' Lene said during a
celebratory family meal. 'You've handled everything
so well!'

'Coach Deila said exactly the same thing,' Martin
replied. 'I can't imagine they'll be throwing a thirteen-
year-old into a first team game, but it'll be special to
see the routine and be around the other players.'

That afternoon, Martin watched with butterflies in
his stomach as Mjøndalen embarrassed Strømsgodset,
taking a 4–0 lead at half-time. It was a very quiet
dressing room, with most players staring at the floor
and shaking their heads. They had all known this was
a tough opponent, but no one had expected to be
pushed around like that.

The Strømsgodset coaches left the players to their

silent misery for a few more minutes, then Coach
Deila tried to lay out a better plan for the second half.

'We're going to make some changes to freshen
things up,' he explained. He pointed to two of the
substitutes who would both be coming on to tighten
up the defence, then he turned to Martin.
'You're coming on too, Martin. We'll get you on the
right wing.'

Martin could feel himself staring. 'Great, yes…
thanks,' he mumbled, rushing to put on his shin pads
and tie his laces. Martin pulled on his navy number 67
shirt and smiled to himself. Surely no other thirteen-
year-old in the world was living this kind of dream.

Hans Erik patted Martin on the back as they walked
out together for the second half. 'Good luck, son,' he
said quietly. 'Show them what you can do.'

As Martin got used to the pace of the game, he was
curious to see how defenders would react to him and
how tightly they would mark him. He soon got his
answer; the Mjøndalen left-back took a couple of quick
steps backwards when Martin turned to face him.

That was an invitation to use the space. Like his dad

had taught him, Martin knew what was in his vicinity, so he took a quick touch inside and glided forward. He dipped his shoulder and floated past two tackles, then looked for the strikers' runs.

He saw Péter darting behind the defence, and he instantly worked out the right angle for a through ball. With one quick flick of his left foot, Martin's pass curled around the nearest defender's outstretched leg. Péter ran onto the pass but was tripped up just before he could shoot. Penalty!

'Great pass, kid,' said Péter, who got up, placed the ball on the spot and scored the penalty.

Though the game finished 5–2 to Mjøndalen, it had given Martin a precious glimpse of what first team life was all about, and he was buzzing as he shook hands at the final whistle. The Mjøndalen players probably wondered why Martin had such a big smile after a loss, but he was too busy enjoying his special moment.

CHAPTER 10

A GREAT EYE FOR GOAL

Before long, Martin felt like part of the team at Strømsgodset. He wasn't just the skinny kid who rocketed up the youth teams anymore. Still, his teammates were quick to protect him on the pitch.

By 2014, Martin wasn't a secret in the Norwegian league. Strømsgodset had made a strong start to the season and were almost unbeatable at home. But the coaches knew that getting Martin on the pitch regularly could take the team to new heights.

After the last training session of the week, Coach Deila appeared next to Martin on his walk back to the main building and walked alongside him.

'I want to talk to you quickly before you go

inside,' he said, giving nothing away with the way his voice sounded.

Martin fidgeted nervously. This could be good news or bad news. But he thought back over the previous few weeks, and could only recall highlights. The biggest of those had come with his league debut – still at just fifteen, and still not a professional player – against Aalesunds on 13 April. That game made him the youngest player ever to participate in a Tippeligaen game.

'Well done again this week,' Coach Deila said. 'Every week, you're adding a little extra to your game and the coaches are all really impressed. We're playing Sarpsborg this weekend, and we'll try to get you some minutes off the bench.'

Martin's legs turned to jelly and, for one scary second, he feared he might fall over. But he recovered just in time to shake Coach Deila's hand. 'Thanks, coach. This means everything to me. I won't let you down.'

Hans Erik drove Martin to the game and tried to crack a few jokes to get him laughing. But Martin was too busy daydreaming about what he would do in his *professional* league debut that afternoon.

As Martin walked onto the pitch to warm up, he was all too aware that he was now playing against grown men. Some players were at least fifteen years older than him, but he had been training with the Strømsgodset first team for long enough not to be bothered by that kind of thing.

He was still getting used to all the fans at Strømsgodset games, though. The Marienlyst Stadion had seats for thousands of supporters, and he could feel the energy of the crowd when he walked along the touchline to the dugout. He waved back when some of the fans called out his name. They could see that Martin was inching closer to playing for the first team and they all wanted to be there to see his firsts: his first game, his first assist, his first goal.

During the first half, Martin got up with the other subs and jogged down towards the corner flag, stretching and watching the game at the same time. With twenty minutes to go, Strømsgodset were winning 2–0 and it was time for some fresh legs.

Coach Deila called the subs back to the dugout, then turned to Martin. 'Ready?' he said.

Martin smiled. 'Always!' he replied.

'Good, you're coming on the next time the ball goes out of play,' Coach Deila said. 'The Sarpsborg defenders look tired, and the game should open up a bit now, so use your pace and run at them.'

The crowd roared and cheered and clapped as Martin took the couple of steps from the dugout to the touchline in his white boots and his Number 16 shirt.

'You'll get no favours from these defenders,' one of the other coaches added just before Martin ran onto the pitch. 'There will be some "welcome to the top division" tackles, but don't lose your cool. Your teammates will have your back out there.'

But none of the Sarpsborg defenders seemed to want to get close enough to Martin to deliver any hard tackles. He could sense their fear any time he turned and ran with the ball, and they were afraid to get too tight to him in case he spun past them.

But giving Martin any room was just as dangerous. His change of direction was so fast, and his feet were so quick. If a defender lunged or fell for one of the fakes, there was usually no way to recover.

Determined to show what he could do, Martin dribbled forward again and again down the right wing – and then in the final minutes of the game, everything clicked. He burst through the Sarpsborg midfield as defenders backed off, and played a quick one-two with striker Péter. Martin got the ball back and there was only one thought in his mind: *shoot.*

He was almost at the edge of the penalty area now, and an angle opened up for him. He drilled a low shot with his left foot and he knew he had hit it well as soon as he felt the connection off his boot. The ball flew towards the bottom corner and into the net, past the goalkeeper's outstretched hand.

Gooooooooooooooooooooaaaaaaaaaaaaaaaaalllllllllllllll llllllllllll!!!!!!!!!!!!!!!!!!!

What a feeling! Martin jogged towards the fans with his arms in the air – and his teammates ran over to celebrate with him.

Back in the dressing room, he was buried in a pile of hugs as every teammate came to shake his hand once again. Many of them said the words that Martin was used to hearing these days: 'I still can't believe you're only fifteen.'

'One day, I'm going to be telling my kids about the day that I set up Martin Ødegaard's first ever goal,' Péter said, laughing. 'I guarantee it!'

Despite all the celebrations and congratulations, Martin was back on the training pitch two days later working as hard as ever. The next step was to move from the bench to the starting line-up, and he was determined to prove that he was ready for a bigger role.

The Strømsgodset coaches were careful with him. In many ways, he was just a boy – he was so much skinnier than the other players in Norway's top league and his body was still growing. He was a substitute for the next two games and got some minutes off the bench, but soon there was no way to keep him out of the team.

After the Strømsgodset players finished a lap of training pitch to warm down, following a practice session, they all went inside to a meeting room, where new boss David Nielsen announced they would face Haugesund at the weekend. Coach Nielsen had been an assistant under Coach Deila, and he knew all about Martin's talent.

'In defence, Marius, Kim and Lars,' Coach Nielsen paused for breath. 'In midfield, Iver, Mohammed, Öyvind and Martin.'

Martin felt his mouth drop open in shock. He would be starting! His whole body was buzzing, and he couldn't stop smiling. Péter reached over to shake his hand. 'You'll be great,' Marius added, patting him on the back.

It was hard for his friends to understand all the emotions rushing through his body. Martin's life these days wasn't like that of many other fifteen-year-olds. But they all hugged him and promised to be there in the crowd for his first start, and Martin did his best to settle the nerves that he could feel building inside him.

On matchday, he kept things as normal as possible. He had his usual breakfast and watched some TV, as if it was any other Saturday – except it wasn't.

Martin did his best to remember every little detail

that day, from the warm-up to the walk out onto the pitch with his teammates to the kick-off. He quickly saw that this was going to be a real battle. Haugesund took the lead, then Iver Fossum made it 1–1.

In the second half, the action raced from one end of the pitch to the other, and that suited Martin just fine. Strømsgodset attacked again and Iver got free in the box. Martin raced forward to support him and Iver spotted his run, laying the ball into his path. Martin was moving so fast that he needed to take a touch to steady himself, but then there was a sea of orange shirts as three defenders rushed to close him down.

It looked like Martin might have missed his best chance to shoot, but he didn't panic. The defenders expected him to use his left foot, but instead he flicked the ball back onto his right foot. That gave him the tiniest of gaps and he smashed a shot into the top corner.

Goooooooooooooooooooaaaaaaaaaaaaaaaallllllllllllll llllllllllll!!!!!!!!!!!!!!!!!!!

'You little genius!' Péter shouted, while the Strømsgodset players crowded round their young star.

It turned out to be the winning goal – and Martin waved proudly to the fans at the final whistle as the players did a lap of the pitch. He had been pulling out all his best moves that afternoon, and he would never get tired of hearing the *oohs* and *aahs* from the crowd when he got the ball.

But Martin saved his very best performance for a match against Lillestrøm later in the season, as the coaches continued to trust him to handle the big-game pressure.

He didn't let them down. A Lillestrøm player slipped near the halfway line and Martin pounced instantly, poking the ball away and dribbling clear. He saw the panic on the defenders' faces as they tried to slow him down, but Martin was flying – and they had no chance once he was moving like that.

He shifted the ball onto his left foot, faked a shot to get another yard of space, and then curled the ball into the net past the diving keeper.

Gooooooooooooooooooooaaaaaaaaaaaaaaaaalllllllllllllll llllllllllll!!!!!!!!!!!!!!!!!!

Then he stunned Lillestrøm again. Öyvind Storflor

broke free, down the left wing, and played the perfect cutback to where Martin was unmarked in the box. Martin was feeling so confident that he didn't even take a touch to control the ball. He just whipped a first-time shot into the net.

Goooooooooooooooooooooaaaaaaaaaaaaaaaaalllllllllllllll llllllllllll!!!!!!!!!!!!!!!!!!!!

Martin raced over to the touchline to celebrate with the coaches and substitutes. Two beautiful goals and it wasn't even half-time yet. When he was playing like this, he really felt like he could do anything when he got the ball.

'You're a joy to watch!' Coach Nielsen said, hugging Martin at the final whistle as Strømsgodset hung on for a 2–1 win. 'Like all the fans, I can't wait to see what you'll do next.'

CHAPTER 11

INTERNATIONAL RECORD-BREAKER

If making his debut at thirteen and scoring his first goal at fifteen wasn't enough, Martin was soon breaking more records – this time for Norway.

One evening, he was finishing his supper when the phone rang on the other side of the room. His mum got up to answer the phone.

'Hello?' Martin heard her say. Then a pause.

'Oh erm, really?' she said. 'Wow!' Then another pause. Lene looked round with a huge smile on her face. 'Martin, it's for you. Do you mind if we put it on speakerphone?'

'What's going on?' Martin asked. He could see that the rest of the family was just as confused.

'Trust me, just take the phone,' Lene added.

'Hello?' he said. He wasn't sure what else to say. He had no idea who he was speaking to.

'Hi, Martin, it's Per-Mathias Høgmo,' the voice said. Martin froze.

In the sudden silence, Per-Mathias added, '…the manager of the Norway national team.'

Martin laughed. 'Sorry, yes, I know who you are. I'm just shocked that you're calling me!'

'Well, I've been following your performances for Strømsgodset, and I can already see that you're going to be a big part of the Norway team for many years,' Per-Mathias went on. 'We want to get you involved as soon as possible, and this friendly against the United Arab Emirates is a great chance for you to link up with the rest of the squad to see what international football is all about. So… well that's it really, I just wanted to tell you personally that you'll be in the squad when I announce it tomorrow.'

Martin looked over at his parents. His mum had her hands over her mouth, with tears in her eyes, and his dad looked like he might cry too.

'Thank you so much,' Martin replied. 'This is a dream come true, and I can't wait to work with you.'

Once the call was over, there were screams of excitement from everyone in the Ødegaard house. 'Just wait until the rest of the world hears about this!' Lene said.

'Oh great, we're going to have to see your face on every football TV show for the next week,' Kristoffer teased, messing up Martin's hair and giving him a big bear hug.

The interview room was packed with reporters for Per-Mathias's press conference to announce the squad. Watching with his family at home, Martin could almost feel the energy through the TV screen. As they had all predicted, the news about Martin immediately went viral. If he played in the friendly, Martin would become Norway's youngest ever international player – and that was all anyone wanted to talk about.

'Martin has played so well in a number of league games that I wanted to see him in the national team,' Per-Mathias explained to reporters. 'I said before the season that he was going to be the comet of this season and that he could become the youngest player in the history of the national team. I am not surprised that he has performed so well up to now. Now I can't wait to see him in action.'

'I like this guy,' Lene said, laughing. 'I can tell he knows what he's talking about!'

Martin laughed. 'Well, I'm happy my parents agree with him! Let's see if everyone else does.' He reached for his phone to check his messages.

It wasn't just the fans that Martin wanted to impress. As he arrived at the hotel to meet up with the rest of the Norway squad, he was still thinking about what kind of welcome he would get from the other players. Would the senior players who spent years proving themselves in the Under 19s and Under 21s be angry that Martin was skipping to the front of the queue like this?

But those fears disappeared as soon as he walked into the team meeting room. If anything, the other players were curious and excited to meet this fifteen-year-old wonderkid that they had heard so much about. Those playing in other leagues in Europe had only seen highlights of Martin.

The senior players in the squad took Martin under their wing and showed him the dos and don'ts. In training, he was usually put in the same group as a couple of the veterans and that made the adjustment easier.

Martin had already flown through the Norway youth teams, usually playing against older boys. The reports from the coaches all brought the same message: this kid is special. In his short time with the Norway Under 16s, he had travelled to Scotland for a tournament and was one of the first names on the team sheet despite only just turning fifteen.

Luckily, Martin was so focused on his football that the high expectations didn't really bother him. He still felt shy around some of the players who he had been watching on TV as a little boy, but he was having too much fun to waste any time thinking about the pressure on his shoulders.

This was just the next step in his whirlwind adventure, and it only took a couple of training sessions to convince Coach Høgmo to put Martin in the starting line-up for the friendly against the United Arab Emirates. His talent was so clear, even alongside the country's best players – how easily he could glide past defenders, how willing he was to try things that might not always work. It was as if he was born to play on the international stage.

Since he got the call-up for the Norway squad, Martin had often wondered what it would be like to put on the shirt and feel like he was representing the whole country. But none of that prepared him for the moment when he saw his shirt hanging up in the dressing room. It was another moment when he just had to pause for a minute to realise where his football journey had taken him over the past few years.

'These defenders won't have played against many wingers like you,' one of the Norway coaches explained, walking next to Martin on the way out for the warm-up. 'Take them on, run at them and force them to make decisions. We'll always have guys in the box ready for a cross.'

Things got even better when Martin actually put the shirt on and looked down at the Norway badge. His heart was racing as he lined up with his teammates in the tunnel, and he felt all kinds of emotions as he sang the national anthem.

With the extra buzz from the anthem, he was straight into the action, taking a corner from the left inside the first two minutes and seeing lots of the ball on the right wing. His movement off the ball was worrying the defenders and he had a good understanding with strikers Fredrik Gulbrandsen and Yann-Erik de Lanlay, even after just a few training sessions.

Any time Norway attacked down the left wing, Martin was ready to run into the box – and that almost got him a debut goal. He guessed that a cross might get past the first defender, and the ball bounced across the box. Martin lunged forward and stretched his right leg as far as it would go. He just couldn't get a good connection on it, and the ball trickled wide. So close!

Martin was determined to show other parts of his game too. He was known for his dribbling and skills, but he worked as hard as any of his teammates that day. He tracked back on the right wing to help the defence, and with a quick burst of energy he was on the attack again at the other end.

That was when Martin was most dangerous. With defenders and midfielders out of position, there was extra space for quick attacks. Martin got the ball and instantly turned away from his marker. There was lots of green space in front of him, and he sprinted forward. He had already spotted Fredrik in the box, and he looped a cross towards him. Fredrik fired a shot towards the net, but the goalkeeper saved it.

Martin never stopped trying to create chances. The next time he got the ball, he decided to go on his own. He turned away from his marker, but his low shot was straight at the keeper.

He hadn't been sure how long he would be on the pitch. It was a friendly, after all, so he expected Coach Høgmo would want to use as many of his substitutes as possible. But Martin was at the heart of all Norway's best moves, and he ended up playing all ninety minutes.

The game ended 0–0 and, as the referee blew the

final whistle, Martin bent over with his hands on his knees. He had used up every little bit of energy, and he walked very slowly towards the dressing room, shaking hands on the way.

'Martin was very close to deciding the game,' Coach Høgmo said in his post-match interview. 'He showed the kind of qualities he has.'

As Martin carefully folded his debut shirt and put it into his bag to add to his collection of important souvenirs, he felt pride running through him again. He was an international footballer now and he was determined to play his part in getting Norway back to the major tournaments.

Playing in a friendly was special, but Martin soon found out that European Championship qualifiers were even better. A few months later, he was standing on the touchline again and coming off the bench for the final twenty-five minutes against Bulgaria. The score was 1–1 and the atmosphere was electric as he heard the fans screaming his name.

When Martin stepped onto the pitch, he became the youngest player ever to play in a European

Championship qualifier, just adding to his list of records. He was soon celebrating with the fans as Norway scored to go 2–1 up.

'I've never seen a stadium rocking like this!' Martin shouted to Stefan Johansen while the players hugged and high-fived near the corner flag.

'Hopefully you'll have lots more nights like this, Martin,' Stefan replied. 'These fans deserve to relive some of the magic years when Norway could match the very best teams.'

Martin nodded, looking around the crowd and seeing the joy and excitement on every face, from an old man in the front row to two kids who might be attending their first game. 'We'll make it happen!' he said, smiling.

CHAPTER 12

CHOOSING BETWEEN THE BIG CLUBS

By now, Martin's rapid rise in European football was no secret. Big clubs around the world were queueing up to convince him that they could offer him the best future, and no one wanted to lose the race for 'the next big thing'.

First, it was just some rumours, and a few stories in the newspaper. Some said that Real Madrid and Barcelona were interested in Martin. Others claimed that Bayern Munich and Manchester City were the likeliest to sign him. Martin, meanwhile, just tried to focus on his football. He was still learning at Strømsgodset and had lots of things he wanted to improve. But soon the rumours turned into visits from scouts and reporters from all over the world.

Some young players might have loved all the

attention that was coming Martin's way, but that had never been his style. He was nervous about all these people coming to see him and how that would impact his teammates and the staff at Strømsgodset. The last thing he wanted was to be a distraction.

'So, which team is here this week?' Péter joked.

'Yeah, I keep thinking we're in the Champions League with all the big clubs in town,' teased Marius.

The Strømsgodset management team knew that their teenage star had outgrown the Norwegian league, and Martin could sense that the clock was ticking too.

Sooner rather than later, he would need to make a difficult decision about his next club – and Real Madrid, Barcelona, Bayern Munich, Borussia Dortmund, Arsenal, Liverpool, Manchester City and countless other teams were waiting patiently to meet with him.

'Don't worry, there's no rush to make a decision,' Hans Erik told him whenever he sensed panic on Martin's face. 'Let's just have the conversations and learn more about your options.'

But nothing could quite prepare Martin for what lay ahead. When he first heard about the list of teams that he and his dad would be speaking with about a possible transfer, he pictured phone calls at their house in Drammen or some meetings in the offices at the Strømsgodset stadium. Instead, Martin got the VIP treatment from the world's biggest clubs, taking his passport and a small suitcase for a whirlwind European tour.

'Mr Ødegaard, follow me please,' said a man in a smart suit and sunglasses. 'The private jet is waiting, and we've got a busy schedule for the next two days.'

Martin looked at his dad, mouth wide open. 'A private jet?' he whispered, unable to hide the huge smile on his face.

'These clubs are all trying to show us how serious they are about signing you,' Hans Erik said. 'I have a feeling we're going to see a lot of this over the next few weeks.'

As they handed over their suitcases and climbed the steps onto the jet, Martin's eyes were popping out of his head. This was a whole different world – leather

seats, a selection of fruit juices, snacks, and a giant
TV screen.

During the following month, Martin spent a lot
of time checking in and out of hotel rooms, shaking
hands with managers or directors of football, and
discussing his future at fancy dinners. Often, he
felt shy, but this was going to be one of the biggest
decisions of his life and he had agreed to meet with
each of the teams on his rather long 'shortlist'.

In their many conversations about this European
adventure, Martin and Hans Erik had come up with
a wishlist for the ideal situation, so that they could
compare all the different offers. But there was one
condition that had to be met: wherever he signed,
Martin had to be part of that club's first team.

Manchester United visited Martin in Norway. He
had already visited the United academy and would
soon speak to Ole Gunnar Solskjær, a United and
Norway legend. Manchester City gave him a tour of
the training ground but stopped short of promising
him a place in the first team.

Arsenal welcomed Martin at a dinner with Arsène

Wenger, where he learned more about the club's history. Meanwhile, Liverpool made a big move of their own, with Steven Gerrard giving Martin and Hans Erik a tour of Anfield.

Bayern Munich and Pep Guardiola also hosted Martin, as did Borussia Dortmund and Jurgen Klopp. In Barcelona, the theme was predictably built around Messi – and he got a tour of the Camp Nou, plus a chance to see Messi play.

In Madrid, Martin sat in a room surrounded by Real's Champions League trophies – and heard all about what it meant to be part of the Real Madrid family. It sounded great, and he was ready to put that option near the top of his list. Then came the clincher. 'When you're not spending time with the first team, we'll continue to develop you with our Castilla team – and we've got Zinedine Zidane coming to manage that team next season,' explained Florentino Pérez, the Real Madrid president.

Martin had been leaning back slightly in his chair and resting his head on the cushioned part at the top, but now he sat up straight. 'Wow! Zidane would be coaching me?' he said suddenly.

'That's right,' said a voice from the doorway.

Martin spun around in his seat and saw Zidane grinning back at him. For a second, he thought he might faint. Zidane was talking to him!

'We're really excited to have him back at the club, and we think he's going to do a fantastic job with our young stars,' Florentino continued, as Martin tried to recover from the surprise.

Still, Martin wanted to take some time to think about everything he had heard on his whirlwind tour. They had a whole folder of notes from all the visits, and it took a few days for Martin and Hans Erik to refresh their memories about who said what in the different meetings.

There was a lot of 'well, Dortmund offered this…' and 'but Barcelona said that…', and Martin still wasn't sure what to do, even after going over all the notes.

Finally, while he and his dad were watching a Spanish league game on TV at home, Martin made his choice.

'Dad, I've thought about it a lot, and I want to go to Real Madrid,' he said.

CHAPTER 13

THE REAL DEAL

'Yes, we're on our way,' the driver explained, speaking on the phone while loading Martin's suitcase into the car in Madrid. 'I see. Okay. We'll come straight there.'

Martin rubbed the sleep from his eyes. The last few weeks had been exhausting, and he had spent all week preparing for the trip. He couldn't wait to get to the hotel to have a nap and a shower – and put on some fresh clothes.

He had a quick nap on the drive from the airport, but he was suddenly wide awake – the car drove into a big car park with Real Madrid signs everywhere. Wait... what?

Martin leaned forward. 'Aren't we stopping at the

hotel first?' he asked, yawning.

'We'll go there afterwards,' the driver replied, with an apologetic smile. 'The timing was going to be too tight – and it wouldn't look good if you were late, would it?'

Before Martin could ask 'Late for what?', the driver was hurriedly opening his door and pointing the way through to the main reception.

Martin looked around in surprise.

'Welcome, Martin!' said a man in a smart suit, shaking his hand and hastening him down a corridor. 'I'm Emilio Butragueño, the director of football at Real Madrid. We were starting to get a little worried! The last few reporters are here now and there's barely a spare seat in the conference room.'

Martin gulped silently. 'Are we doing the press conference now?' he asked, panic all over his face. He looked down at what he was wearing and wished he could run out to the car to get his suitcase. But he was out of time.

More Real Madrid staff were walking over now, shaking hands, explaining how things would work and listing the types of questions to expect. One woman passed him a pair of headphones and told him that any questions in Spanish would be translated into his ear so he could understand them and then answer in English.

Martin tried to concentrate but his head was spinning.

It was an even bigger shock for him when he walked into the room. There were cameras everywhere. Rows and rows of people looked up at him, though he was relieved to see there were some reporters from Norway that he knew. It would have been a lot for any player to handle, but it was especially terrifying for a sixteen-year-old.

Still, this was part of the job now. He could still be himself, but he would be seeing a lot of microphones in the years ahead, with everyone desperate to get his thoughts on Real Madrid, the transfer, the future and more. His dad had assured him that Real Madrid would probably give him some help so that speaking with reporters felt more natural.

After Emilio's brief introduction, Martin heard

the first question in his headphones. He looked up nervously. 'It's a dream come true, it's unbelievable and it's incredible,' he answered. 'I'm ready for the best club in the world.'

With each question, Martin felt himself relax a little and smile more. Then there was some movement in the corner of the room and a man passed a Real Madrid shirt to Emilio, who unfolded it to show the name 'Ødegaard' on the back. He and Martin stood up, each holding one sleeve of the shirt, and the cameras flashed again and again.

When Martin was back in the car and finally on the way to his hotel, he took a deep breath and leaned back against the headrest. One of the hardest parts was done. He was still nervous about meeting all the Real Madrid players, but he also felt a jolt of excitement when he thought about practising alongside so many amazing footballers.

'I think I need someone to pour a bucket of cold water over my head,' Martin suggested as he told Kristoffer about his first day of Real Madrid training. 'It was like someone picked me up and dropped me in the middle of this football dream where I was playing with the best players in the world.'

Kristoffer laughed. 'For most people that would be a dream, but that's your life now,' he said. 'I'd still love to be the one to pour the water on you though!'

It was clear that Martin had entered a whole new world. While he was being driven to training by his dad, the Real Madrid car park was packed with the most expensive cars that money could buy. Everywhere he looked, he saw designer clothes, expensive shoes, shiny watches and all the latest electronics. Being part of Real Madrid was the high point of any player's career – so how was he supposed to adapt to all of this as a sixteen-year-old? There was no guidebook for this kind of change.

Martin would be getting Spanish lessons over the next few months – but until then, the club suggested that some of the English speakers at the club could help him adapt to life at Real.

'That'll be really helpful, thanks,' he told the Real representatives who were helping him get settled. He assumed that meant the team's translator or someone in the media team. But he almost fell to the floor when those English speakers turned out to be Cristiano Ronaldo and Luka Modrić.

'Welcome to Real!' Luka said, shaking his hand. 'We've heard a lot about you.'

'I know what it's like to move to a new country at a young age, and you're even younger than I was when I joined Manchester United,' Cristiano added. 'We'll do our best to make things easier for you and help you get settled in Madrid.'

'The coaches told us that you'll be joining the first-team training,' Luka continued, while Martin felt his head spinning in the company of such famous players. 'This is going to be fun!'

Martin would never get tired of joining in with his new teammates to flick the ball around in a circle, as they all tried to outdo each other with outrageous skill and control. Cristiano effortlessly balanced the ball on the back of his neck, then looped it up down to his foot. Karim Benzema controlled the ball on his shoulder, then whipped it across the circle with his heel.

In the past, sometimes Martin had been shy about doing his tricks in front of his teammates in case he looked like a show-off, but there was no danger of that here. From the warm-up to the five-a-side games at the end of the sessions, it was skills, skills and more skills at Real.

As always, Martin was quiet in the dressing room and in team meetings, but he came alive when he had a ball at his feet. Even Cristiano and Sergio Ramos whistled and clapped when he fizzed a volley into the top corner with his first attempt of a shooting drill.

'I like your style!' Cristiano said, high-fiving Martin as he jogged to the back of the line.

Martin already knew that he wouldn't be getting many minutes with the first team – and a few weeks of training sessions showed him how much work he still had to do to play regularly at this level. But Real had made plans to make sure he wasn't spending his time getting bored watching from the crowd.

For now, Martin would continue to train with the first team three times a week, learning from Cristiano and Luka, and then he would join up with Castilla, the

Real B team, for games at the weekend.

Castilla played in Real Madrid kits too, and while preparing for a B team game against Barakaldo, Martin found himself staring at the famous club badge. It might not have all the luxury of life in the first team, but he knew that the Real coaches and scouts would be watching closely – and he still couldn't believe that his Castilla boss was Zinedine Zidane!

'Listen up, guys,' Zidane said, appearing in the doorway of the dressing room. 'Barakaldo are going to be physical, and they've got some quality up front. But if we move the ball, we're going to create chances. Don't wait for an invitation. Attack from the start.'

Martin jumped up and down, hearing the familiar sound of his studs tapping on the floor. Out on the pitch, he went through a few more stretches and passed the ball back and forth with one of the Castilla strikers, Raúl de Tomás.

Castilla followed Zidane's words and took every opportunity to push forward. After just eight minutes, Raúl got behind the defence and three Barakaldo defenders rushed back to block his path. Martin sprinted forward into a big gap to his right.

'Raúl, lay it off!' he yelled, panting as he ran.

Martin didn't even need to slow down as the pass arrived. He glanced up to see where the goalkeeper was, then chipped the ball over him and into the net.

Goooooooooooooooooooooaaaaaaaaaaaaaaaaaallllllllllllll lllllllllllll!!!!!!!!!!!!!!!!!!!!!

It wasn't the hardest goal he had ever scored but it meant a lot to get his first goal in the famous white shirt. His Castilla teammates ran over with high-fives and they cruised through the rest of the game, winning 4–0.

Back in the dressing room, Martin put his shirt on the bench next to him and grinned as he thought about the last few months. Life didn't get much better than this!

CHAPTER 14

CASTILLA HIGHS AND LOWS

In the early days in Madrid, there were a lot of laughs to go with the excitement of practising with the best players in the world and learning from Zidane at Castilla. But as the months passed, the adventure started to feel a little less like a dream.

'It's just… well, I don't really feel part of either team,' Martin admitted as he spoke to Kristoffer one afternoon. 'I feel stuck and I'm not playing anywhere near my best with Castilla.'

At first, it had seemed like a perfect arrangement, but he quickly began to feel unsettled. Everyone was nice with him, but he couldn't shake the feeling that the Real Madrid first-team players must be wondering why he was there – and the Castilla players must be wondering why he was so special that he didn't need to train with them during the week.

'If it's not working, you should talk to some of the coaches to get their thoughts,' Kristoffer suggested. 'Maybe it's time for the club to choose which path to put you on, at least for the next year or two.'

Martin promised to think about that. In many ways, there was no better place to be for a young footballer and his Castilla teammates were all so talented. But when he watched the highlights of his games, it was clear to him that he didn't have the same connection as the players who trained together with Castilla.

Martin would make a good run, but his teammates weren't expecting it. Then he would cut inside just as one of the strikers was dropping deep – and they would almost collide with each other. Even though he had some flashes of genius, with a mazy dribble or a change of direction that left a defender on the floor, Martin knew his performances didn't lead to goals often enough. The pressure grew as Castilla lost four matches in a row.

Partway through the season, Martin joined up with the Norway squad and had to miss a Castilla game. When he returned, he found himself on the bench. 'We're going to stick with the team that won the last game,' Zidane explained. 'But stay ready and we'll get you on.'

It would have been easy for Martin to sulk – but he didn't. He cheered on his teammates and kept a smile on his face. But it was still hard to ignore the reports and whispers about the wonderkid who couldn't get a game for the B team.

'I'm not a quitter,' Martin told his dad at lunch that week. 'I'm going to keep fighting and I know I can play a lot better.'

His patience and hard work were rewarded at the very end of the 2014–15 season when Carlo Ancelotti named Martin in the Real squad for the final league game at home to Getafe. Maybe, just maybe, he would get to make his first team debut.

'I don't want to get my hopes up and then be disappointed if I just have to watch from the bench,' he told siblings Emilie and Mari on the phone. 'But cross your fingers for me!'

As Martin warmed up along the touchline, the fans cheered loudly. He gave them a shy wave back. Like them, he had no idea if he would get any minutes that afternoon, but Real were winning easily and that seemed like a promising sign.

In the second half, one of the coaches signalled for him to come back from the corner flag where he was doing more stretches. Martin jogged over, trying to play it cool.

The coach put his arm on Martin's shoulder and then opened a folder with some instructions. 'You're coming on for Cristiano and we'll move you over to the right wing,' he explained, pointing to one of the sheets in the folder. Martin nodded, his heart thumping louder and louder in his chest.

A long Getafe clearance flew into the stands. The referee blew his whistle and turned towards the touchline, making the substitution sign with his hands.

'Here we go!' Martin said quietly to himself. Carlo gave him a quick good-luck handshake, and the crowd clapped first Cristiano, then Martin.

'Enjoy it!' Cristiano said, giving Martin a hug. 'You'll never forget this moment.'

Martin looked all around the Bernabéu Stadium as he ran onto the pitch. He saw a sea of white shirts, with everyone on the edge of their seats ready to see the young star they had heard so much about over the past two years.

He laughed to himself. Sometimes that was all he could do. This story – his story – was like something from a film. He was a sixteen-year-old from a small town in Norway and he had just replaced Cristiano Ronaldo to make his debut for Real Madrid.

Martin was going into the history books again too with another new record – the youngest player to play for Real Madrid. The game had slowed down and he got lots of early touches. As it was the last game of the season, no one was flying into tackles, and he drifted inside to play one-twos and quick layoffs. He played a little reverse pass that almost set up a chance, but the offside flag went up.

He was easy to see in his bright red boots, and the

Bernabéu crowd cheered every time he got the ball. They could see how comfortable he was and how easily he found space between the midfield and defence.

Martin worked harder than ever over the summer to get himself in top condition for the 2016–17 season. With a fresh start looming, he was determined to show the improvements in his game. He was back in the Castilla team but the path to regular games for the Real Madrid first team felt just as challenging as it had done twelve months earlier, even though he made his first start for the first team in the Spanish cup.

Eventually, all the uncertainty started to really affect Martin. He wanted to play first-team football, and it had become clear that he would need to move to get that. He and Hans Erik arrived at the Real Madrid training ground early one morning and walked through the main building. Together, in a meeting with the club's directors, the two of them explained how Martin was feeling and why a loan move felt like the right next step.

After some difficult conversations, Real agreed. But,

with the slow progress in his time in Spain, there was a very different reaction from the last time he was available. There were certainly no private jets this time. Martin waited patiently to see what offers he got, and then decided to join Heerenveen in the Dutch league on an eighteen-month loan.

'Here we go!' Martin said, after signing all the forms. 'People say that change can be good. I hope they're right!'

CHAPTER 15

WORKING HARD AT HEERENVEEN

'Welcome to Heerenveen, Martin!' the reporter said to him, while they sat together in one of the club's interview rooms.

'It's good to be here,' Martin replied, smiling a little nervously at the TV cameras pointing in his direction.

Suddenly there was a knock on the door. Martin looked over at the club's interviewer, who just shrugged and got up to see who it was.

'Sorry to interrupt,' said a voice from the corridor that Martin immediately recognised as his new teammate, Morten Thorsby. 'But, Martin, we can't let you walk to training every day or take the bus.'

Martin laughed. 'What's going on out there?' he called, hearing thudding sounds as if someone was banging into the wall.

'Well, we just wanted to do something to make life a bit easier until you're old enough to get your driver's licence,' Morten shouted from the corridor.

Then he paused, and Martin looked up to see Morten riding into the room on a shiny new bike. He burst out laughing.

'Come on, let's see those cyclist hand signals – turning left, turning right,' Morten joked.

Martin knew he would need to pass his driving test, but until then the bike was an amazing present, and just the latest thing that his new team had done to make him feel at home.

Even so, joining Heerenveen halfway through the season was a strange feeling. He had to learn names, directions and tactics in a hurry so that he could make the most of his time on the pitch. He still wasn't sure what would happen next with Real Madrid, but he wasn't about to change the way he played. He wanted to attack, take some risks with the ball and entertain the fans.

The Heerenveen coaches gave him their full support. 'That's exactly what we want from you – those magic moments,' manager Jurgen Streppel said during one training session. 'There are very few players who can change a game in an instant like you can.'

But Martin got off to a slow start and it was frustrating to read stories about how he was running out of time to get his career back on track. 'Do they realise that I'm still only eighteen?' he asked his dad, half joking, half angry. 'Could I at least play a few seasons before people write me off?'

As he prepared for the 2017–18 season, Martin felt more confident – and he had turned some of his frustration into extra motivation.

'This season is going to be a different story,' Martin told his dad during a walk near the Heerenveen stadium. 'They're all going to see the real me once I have a full pre-season with my teammates.'

Hans Erik had moved with Martin to Heerenveen

to make sure that he didn't have to go through this move alone, and it had really helped to have him there.

'My goal is still the same – to earn a place in the Real Madrid first team,' Martin continued. 'But I know I need to be playing regularly to develop my game.'

Warming up with Morten and Denzel Dumfries before a game against FC Twente, Martin was still looking for his first league goal for Heerenveen. His passes had set up plenty of goals for his teammates, but he could think of at least three or four times when he had been denied by great saves. Maybe his luck would finally change today.

'Keep making those runs,' Denzel said, as Morten nodded next to him. 'That first goal is coming.'

Martin mostly stayed out wide on the right wing, but he sometimes crept inside to a more central position when the ball was on the other side of the pitch. During one of those moments, he saw a long ball over the top causing panic in the FC Twente defence. The keeper reacted quickly to sprint out to the edge of his box, but his clearance was disastrous. It landed straight at Martin's feet about twenty-five yards out.

Martin's eyes lit up. In that split second, he told himself not to rush it, but the pace on the ball was perfect for him to loft a shot into the empty net.

Gooooooooooooooooooooaaaaaaaaaaaaaaaaalllllllllll llllllllllllllll!!!!!!!!!!!!!!!!!!!!

Finally! Martin jogged over to the Heerenveen fans and soaked up the cheers. 'I guess our prediction was right!' Morten shouted, hugging Martin.

That goal seemed to unlock more of his magic. His Strømsgodset moves were back – the reverse passes, the quick feet to weave past defenders, the ball glued to his foot like a magnet. Martin had a gift for seeing things a step ahead. While some players would control a pass, look up, consider the different options, take another touch and miss out on opportunities to unlock a defence, it was all instant with Martin. He knew exactly what he wanted to do before the ball even reached him.

After the final home game of the season, all Martin's excitement was replaced with a strange, uneasy feeling. He sat down to clear out his locker and packed up his shoes, socks and other clothes. Just like that, his loan spell was over. He would always remember his Heerenveen experience and there was a lot of sadness as he said goodbye to teammates who had become good friends.

As for next season, that was still a big mystery.

CHAPTER 16

SUCCESS WITH VITESSE

The situation was no different when Martin spoke with Real Madrid that summer. The team was competing for trophies and there was still a handful of players ahead of him in the queue. So, he had a choice to make: be an occasional player for Real or go out on loan again. That was an easy decision for someone who was at his happiest when he was playing every week.

After more discussions, Real agreed another loan deal – again in the Dutch league, but this time with Vitesse. Martin got a good feeling about it straightaway.

'Your spark is back,' Hans Erik said after Martin's first few weeks with Vitesse. 'I can see it in the way you move and the way you talk to your teammates. It was starting to return at Heerenveen, but this month has reminded me of watching you at Strømsgodset, or even Drammen Strong. You believe you can score every time you get the ball, or create a chance for someone else.'

Martin nodded. 'No more playing it safe,' he said.

Away to Heracles Almelo, Martin gave Vitesse fans a glimpse of what they could expect. A long, overhit cross came all the way from the left wing over to Martin on the right. He had to readjust to control the looping ball and two defenders backed off as he turned inside. That was enough of an invitation for him. He danced forward with two quick touches to open up space for a shot. He struck the ball exactly how he wanted to – with lots of whip and curl.

The goalkeeper had no chance as the rocket shot flew into the top corner.

*Gooooooooooooooooooooaaaaaaaaaaaaaaaallllllllllllll
llllllllllll!!!!!!!!!!!!!!!!!!!!*

What a way for Martin to introduce himself to the Vitesse fans! He could hear the supporters in the away end of the stadium singing his name.

'That's what I'm talking about,' Vitesse winger Bryan Linssen said, hugging Martin. 'You can change a game with three touches.'

But Martin was just getting started. That goal gave him even more confidence to try tricks and flicks to keep defenders guessing. Against Utrecht, he was at the heart of all the team's attacks and grabbed the ball immediately when Vitesse won a free kick twenty-five yards out. No one argued.

He placed the ball and whispered with two teammates just to try to confuse the Utrecht wall about who was taking the free kick. The referee blew the whistle and Martin took a two-step run-up before fizzing a curling shot over the wall and into the net. The goalkeeper didn't even move.

Goooooooooooooooooooooaaaaaaaaaaaaaaaaaalllllllllllllll llllllllllll!!!!!!!!!!!!!!!!!!!!

'Do you ever score ugly goals?' Bryan joked, running over to celebrate with Martin.

By now, Martin was a favourite with the Vitesse crowd. He was the type of player that they had been waiting for the club to sign.

'The Vitesse coaches have put their trust in me , and I'm trying to pay them back by playing at my best,' Martin told his mum and his sisters on a weekend video call. 'So far, it's going really well.'

Away at Kozakken Boys, Martin was the hero again. With the score locked at 1–1, there were tired players all over the pitch, but Martin still had an extra burst of energy. With almost ninety-two minutes on the clock, he looked up and saw he was just about in shooting range. It was worth a try. He steadied himself and fired a low shot between two defenders.

It wasn't his best effort – or his hardest. But the placement couldn't have been better. The ball arrowed towards the bottom corner, past the goalkeeper's outstretched hand and into the net.

Goooooooooooooooooooooaaaaaaaaaaaaaaaaaallllllllllllll llllllllllll!!!!!!!!!!!!!!!!!!

Martin set off running. His Number 18 shirt was just a blur as his tired teammates raced to catch up with him.

Somehow, Martin still found ways to surprise his

teammates with a new piece of skill or a new turn that he had been working on. Sometimes it worked, sometimes it didn't. Away at FC Emmen, he sensed another opportunity to try something different. When Vitesse won a free kick over by the touchline on the right wing, he lined it up and watched the crowd of players battling for position just inside the penalty area.

He also spotted the FC Emmen goalkeeper taking a few steps off his line to get into a better position to catch the ball as it curled into the box. After all, the angle for the free kick was so tight that no one would think to shoot from there.

Well, almost no one. Martin gave nothing away as he took a few steps backwards, then he ran up to the ball and whipped a shot towards the wide-open space at the unguarded near post. A second too late, the goalkeeper saw what was happening. But his feet wouldn't move fast enough. The ball floated towards the net and crept just inside the post.

Goooooooooooooooooooooaaaaaaaaaaaaaaaaalllllllllllllll llllllllllll!!!!!!!!!!!!!!!!!!

'Are you kidding me?!' Max called, laughing. 'That's ridiculous!'

'You're the only person I know who would try to score from there!' Bryan added, jumping on Martin's back.

The Vitesse experience was everything Martin had hoped it would be, and he kept up his scoring form in the summer with his first goal for Norway in a draw against Romania. Martin was getting used to taking his football one year at a time, but one thing was clear – his career trajectory was rising again.

CHAPTER 17

BACK TO SPAIN WITH SOCIEDAD

Back in Madrid, though, the same challenges were still standing in Martin's way, even though he had been hopeful about turning things around. There were so many star players at the club, especially in midfield, and the coaches were honest about how much time he might spend on the bench.

These were the tough moments. 'I've done the loan moves, I've spent seasons in different cities and I'm getting nowhere,' he told his mum one evening. 'I'm not sure if I'll ever get another chance here.'

For the first time, Martin really couldn't see where his career was going. But he felt better when he heard that clubs were still interested in him, including Real

Sociedad who were offering him a two-year loan deal to stay in La Liga.

Though Martin didn't love the idea of packing his suitcases again and moving into a hotel or a short-term home in another new place, he realised this might be the new chapter that unlocked the rest of his career.

'I've thought about this a lot over the last few days and I think Real Sociedad is a great fit for me,' Martin told his family, with what he hoped was a confident grin. 'I really want to stay in Spain and show everyone what I can do.'

When he spoke to the Sociedad coaches, Martin could sense that he would have every chance to win a regular place in the team, and he settled quickly into his first training session. It definitely helped that he had been through the awkward introduction phase during his other loan moves, so he wasn't as shy about getting to know his new teammates.

Martin made himself even more popular by being a regular goalscorer for Sociedad, starting with the winning goal against Malaga. It was a classic Martin goal, timing his run perfectly, taking a touch to get beyond the last defender and then placing an unstoppable shot past the keeper.

Goooooooooooooooooooaaaaaaaaaaaaaaaaallllllllllllll llllllllllll!!!!!!!!!!!!!!!!!!!!!

'The fans love you already!' Mikel Oyarzabal shouted as they ran together to the corner flag. They had built an instant connection on the pitch, with Martin always looking for his runs down the left wing.

Martin was enjoying the freedom to roam inside from the right wing, linking with striker Alexander Isak. But the Sociedad coaches were also happy for him to drift into central positions at times and almost become another striker.

Martin found himself doing exactly that against Atlético Madrid. Mikel Merino burst forward on the left, catching the Atlético defence by surprise, and Martin darted across the pitch to give him an option on the edge of the box.

Merino saw Martin and pinged the ball towards him. Now it was Martin's turn to feel crowded as two defenders appeared to close him down, but he danced away from their hesitant tackles and whipped a left-footed shot towards the far corner. Though it wasn't his best shot, the ball took a little deflection and spun into the net.

Goooooooooooooooooooaaaaaaaaaaaaaaaaaalllllllllllllll llllllllllll!!!!!!!!!!!!!!!!!!!!

Martin ran off with his arms in the air and his teammates chased after him, pulling him down and jumping on top of him. Sociedad were heading for another win.

Even Hans Erik had to admit that he was seeing another layer to Martin's game at Sociedad. Those early goals seemed to have given him more confidence – and once he got going, he looked like the young superstar that so many had predicted he would become.

Any time he pulled back his left foot for a shot or a pass, good things happened. Against Alavés, Martin played the pass of the season, giving Oyarzabal a tap-in with a beautiful curling assist that left two defenders looking at each other in shock. It would have been so easy to hit the pass a little too hard or a little too softly. But Martin had judged it effortlessly.

'How did you even see that angle?' Alexander asked. 'You're a cheat code!'

Sociedad were one of the biggest surprise stories in Spain, and Martin kept a close eye on the league table. No one seemed to have picked Sociedad to start so strongly.

Another date that he had circled on his calendar was a Copa del Rey clash with Real Madrid. Sociedad were clear underdogs, but there was immediately something special for Martin about being back at the Bernabéu. He saw all the usual sights and smelled all the usual smells. This place had been his home – and it might still be again one day.

But that night he had a job to do for Sociedad – and there was the added motivation of showing Real Madrid what they were missing. As he looked across the pitch at kick-off, he saw the familiar faces of Sergio Ramos and Toni Kroos. He had learned so much from them, and for the next ninety minutes he had to show he could reach their level.

Sociedad manager Imanol Alguacil had said all week that sitting back and playing defensively would give

Real too much freedom. 'We have to be willing to take some chances,' he explained. 'Martin and Mikel – that means getting forward to support Alexander.'

In the first half, a rushed clearance landed at Alexander's feet and he sped away. With defenders closing in, he took a long-range shot and the Real Madrid keeper dived to push the ball clear.

But Martin was in the right place at the right time. The ball deflected straight to him at the edge of the penalty area, and he was on it in a flash. Before anyone else could react, he fired in a low shot that nutmegged a defender and the keeper.

Goooooooooooooooooooooaaaaaaaaaaaaaaaaalllllllllllllll llllllllllll!!!!!!!!!!!!!!!!!!

The Bernabéu went silent. Martin wasn't sure whether he should celebrate against the club that had loaned him to Sociedad in the first place, so instead he just waited for his teammates to swarm round him.

It was just one of those days when everything worked for Sociedad. Alexander scored two goals in three minutes in the second half, and they survived a nervy finish to win 4–3.

'You guys deserved that tonight,' Toni admitted, hugging Martin and wishing him good luck for the next round. 'It's good to see you enjoying your football.'

'How could you do that to us?!' Sergio said, pretending to be angry with Martin before putting an arm round him.

Martin joined his Sociedad teammates to applaud their fans in the far end of the stadium. It felt good to come back to Madrid and prove a point. It was just one game, but he was really pleased with his performance.

'Let's enjoy this one tonight,' Imanol told his players as the celebrations started in the dressing room. 'But we've got more big tests ahead, and this performance showed we can beat anyone on our day.'

With Martin playing some of his best football, Sociedad finished sixth and qualified for the Europa League. But just as everything was clicking into place, life became complicated again.

CHAPTER 18

ARSENAL'S NEW MIDFIELD MAESTRO

While Martin took a well-deserved summer break, Real Madrid made it clear that they wanted him back at the Bernabéu to be part of preseason training, skipping the second year of the loan deal with Real Sociedad. Zidane was managing the Real Madrid first team now and he called Martin to confirm that he was part of his plans.

But Martin wasn't sure if there was really any unfinished business for him in Madrid, and he was soon pacing the room and questioning the decision. There was so much competition for the starting line-up at Real Madrid and he could hardly argue about being a backup behind superstars like Luka and Toni.

Then Martin was ill for a few weeks. He returned to work too soon and knew he wasn't at his best. That just made things worse. In the spring of 2020, when the global health crisis shut down leagues around the world, it turned into the most unusual season ever. But Martin suddenly had more time to think – about his time in Madrid and what he wanted to do next. At some point, he would have to accept that things just weren't going to work out at Real Madrid, and that was okay.

'I can't keep doing this with Real,' he told Kristoffer. 'I'm going round and round in circles. I'm not sure where I'll end up next, but I think I need to hit the reset button and move on. People talk about me like I'm in my thirties, but I'm only twenty-one. I've got my best years ahead of me on the pitch.'

Kristoffer nodded. He had watched his brother battle for a chance in Madrid and knew how exhausting that had been. 'Whatever you decide, we'll support you 100 per cent,' he said. 'There are lots of other great clubs out there and a fresh start could be really good for you.'

After the ups and downs at Real Madrid, followed by three different loan moves, Martin knew that he needed to get his next decision right. He still loved playing football – it was a dream job. But he wanted to find a new club that felt like home.

Again, there were different options to consider, but one team jumped off the screen when Martin saw the list. Arsenal wanted him!

Martin remembered his visit with Arsenal as a teenager. He had good memories of his time in London and meeting Arsène Wenger. It was the simplest decision of his life to agree to meet with Mikel Arteta, the Arsenal manager. With such limited travel during the health crisis, Martin received a link for a video call and tidied up behind him to make sure there was no mess in the background.

He sat down, took a deep breath and joined the meeting. A few seconds later, Mikel's face appeared on the screen.

'Well, I'm not sure I'll ever get used to meeting players like this,' Mikel joked, repositioning his camera. 'But I'm so happy we're getting to talk. I've followed your career closely and I know it's not been easy the past few years. You've handled the ups and downs really well, though.'

'Thanks,' Martin said, grinning. He knew it was true, but it was still nice to hear. 'It definitely feels like I've been on one long rollercoaster since I was sixteen, but I'm determined to stay on the ride.'

Mikel laughed. 'Well, you have my promise that we'll do our best to make this next part less bumpy. We know how talented you are, and this timing could be perfect.'

When Martin asked about the project at Arsenal, the conversation got even more exciting.

'Our young core is incredible,' Mikel said. 'I don't think most people know how special these kids are yet, but soon it'll be clear to everyone. What we need is another midfield playmaker who can control the game and make everyone better. I know you're still young, but you've got a lot of experience to bring to the dressing room.'

By the time the call ended, Martin had no doubts. 'I could have signed for Arsenal all those years ago,' he told his parents that night. 'Maybe that's where I was always meant to be.'

The signature was only just dry on the contract when Mikel gave Martin the news. 'We're going to throw you straight into the squad to play Manchester United,' he explained, grinning. 'Don't worry, you can learn everyone's name during the warm-up!'

Martin watched excitedly from the bench as Arsenal battled Manchester United, two of the great Premier League teams that he had watched on TV back in Drammen. This was his kind of football, and it just made him even happier with his decision to come to England.

The more Martin trained with his new teammates, the more he learned about how Mikel wanted Arsenal to play – the pressing, the direct style, the fast pace. Walking around the pitch with Bukayo Saka before a Europa League game against Olympiacos, Martin was really feeling at home in England and he loved these big away games, even if the atmosphere wasn't the same without the fans in the stands.

That night, he found lots of space in midfield.

Thomas Partey clipped a quick pass to him, and Martin saw that no one was closing him down. He saw that the strikers were being marked closely, so he dribbled on towards the edge of the box and smashed an unstoppable shot that dipped and swerved past the Olympiacos keeper.

Goooooooooooooooooooooaaaaaaaaaaaaaaaaalllllllllllllll llllllllllll!!!!!!!!!!!!!!!!!!!!

What a feeling! Martin always believed that he could test a keeper on his left foot from that kind of distance, and the rest of the Arsenal players wrapped him in hugs before he could even think of a goal celebration.

He couldn't wait to experience a North London derby, and he didn't have to wait long. Tottenham took the lead, but Martin was finding pockets of space. Kieran Tierney raced clear on the left and Martin made his move. He delayed his run slightly and no one followed him. The cross was perfect, but Martin scuffed his shot. He looked up expecting to see the ball easily saved, but somehow it confused the Tottenham keeper and trickled into the corner.

Goooooooooooooooooooooaaaaaaaaaaaaaaaaallllllllllllll llllllllllll!!!!!!!!!!!!!!!!!!!

Martin sprinted off and slid on his knees. Arsenal were back in the game and he kept pushing forward, sensing that Tottenham were wobbling. Sure enough, Alexandre Lacazette scored the winner in the second half, and Martin could almost picture what it would have been like if the Arsenal fans had been jumping and dancing in the away end of the stadium.

'That should give the fans something to cheer about at home,' he said to Bukayo as they all celebrated the win in a noisy dressing room.

While Martin prepared to enjoy some time in the sun over the summer, he crossed his fingers and hoped that Arsenal and Real Madrid could reach some kind of agreement for him to stay in London. The last few months had been amazing, and he wasn't ready to leave.

CHAPTER 19

NORWAY'S NEW CAPTAIN FANTASTIC

Martin knew the stories about Norway's struggles to reach major international tournaments – his family and friends talked about it all the time. After reaching the 1994 and 1998 World Cups and Euro 2000, the Norwegians were now experiencing a big-time drought. It had been more than twenty years since they last took part in a major tournament, but there were hopes that this latest group of youngsters could turn their fortunes around.

Even at twenty-two years old, Martin was an established member of the national team. Since his record-breaking debut, he had been a regular in the team, but Norway had faced some difficult years with disappointing results. On the positive side, there were lots of good young players coming through and getting used to international football.

There had been some big changes lately too. Ståle Solbakken had been appointed as the new Norway boss, former captain Stefan Johansen had retired, and young goal-machine Erling Haaland had burst onto the scene. The new era had big potential.

Martin was excited to see Coach Solbakken's approach and to find out what the squad would look like ahead of a busy year of World Cup qualifiers. Would it be a similar group of players, or would there be some surprises?

What he didn't know yet was that one of the biggest surprises would be about him. Norway needed a new captain, and Coach Solbakken decided Martin's quiet leadership made him the right choice to take over the armband.

Martin was speechless. It wasn't something he had expected, and it felt like an incredible honour that he was being trusted to lead the team forward. Now he really had to deliver. But their path to qualifying for the 2022 World Cup was going to be tough, with Holland and Turkey also in their group.

Norway got off to a winning start against Gibraltar, but a 3–0 loss to Turkey showed that there was still a lot of work to be done. Even with Martin playing well and Erling looking like a future superstar, the team wasn't fully clicking yet.

As the players stretched on the pitch before a game against the Netherlands, Martin went round to see each of his teammates, patting them all on the shoulder and giving them a positive message about what they meant to the team.

'Well, you know what you need to do, big man, so I won't even bother saying it,' Martin told Erling. They both laughed.

'Must... score... goals,' Erling replied, pretending to be a robot.

Sure enough, Erling scored to put Norway ahead. But they were pegged back to 1–1 before half-time.

In the second half, Martin was everywhere in midfield, racing forward to link up with Erling, then charging back to help protect the defence. Then he won the ball and spotted a chance to counterattack. There were wide open spaces in front of him and he didn't hesitate. The Netherlands players couldn't keep up with him. With the last defender off balance, Martin slid a quick pass through to Erling, who took a touch and then crashed a shot against the crossbar.

'Aaaaaaaah!' Martin screamed, with his hands on his head. If the shot had been a few inches lower, it would have been a certain goal.

Norway had to settle for a draw, though it was a good point to add to their total in the group table, and Martin and Erling had shown the potential in their partnership.

But a loss and a draw from their last two group games left Norway in third place. They missed out on the World Cup playoffs and would have to watch another big tournament from home. This one really stung and he could see disappointment expressions all around the dressing room.

Martin allowed his teammates some quiet moments, then he stood up. One by one, the other players looked over at him. 'Boys, I know this hurts, but let's remember we're heading in the right direction,' he said. 'Once we really hit top gear, we'll show the world what Norway is capable of.'

That changed the mood a little. There were hugs, high-fives and promises to put things right for the next World Cup. Martin gave Erling a fist bump as they headed for the team bus.

'The best is yet to come,' Martin said, with the best grin he could manage.

CHAPTER 20

THE YOUNG GUNNERS

Ever since leaving Strømsgodset, Martin had been searching for a new home – somewhere he felt settled and could see himself staying for a long time. Arsenal had felt right from the very start.

Things were rarely simple when it came to Martin's football career, though. At first, Real Madrid made it clear that they wanted him to return once again for preseason training. Martin did as he was told, but soon found a moment to sit down with new boss Carlo Ancelotti to explain why he thought it was time for him to move on from Real Madrid – for good.

Eventually, his wish was granted, and that decision would resume conversations with Arsenal. It was time to fully close the Real Madrid chapter and Martin was soon signing a four-year contract to join the Gunners on a permanent deal.

Mikel's project would take some time, and Martin was ready to help lead it forward. But he also knew that Arsenal had been out of the Premier League title picture for too long. The fans were desperate for success, to get behind a new team of heroes and relive the magic of Wenger's best years.

Arsenal were a young team – and young teams usually struggled to be consistent. Some months, they looked like they would never lose again, and other months they seemed to forget how to defend or score. But Mikel never lost patience or focus – and that gave Martin confidence.

He could feel his own game rising and rising, and he could see the improvements throughout the squad. Bukayo Saka was so quick and so direct, Granit Xhaka covered so much ground in midfield and Pierre-Emerick Aubameyang and Alexandre Lacazette could both score spectacular goals.

But it was a rocky start to the 2021–22 season for

Arsenal, beginning with a 5–0 loss to Manchester City. After all the preseason buzz, Martin trudged off the pitch full of disappointment. If the Gunners were going to compete for trophies, he knew they had to find a way to get to City's level.

He did his best to put that result out of his mind and focus on the next tests. Away to Burnley, Martin slipped a pass into Bukayo's path but was tripped as he sprinted towards the penalty area. It was a free kick in a dangerous position and Martin hurried over to join the conversation with Thomas and Pierre-Emerick about who would take it.

All three of them stood around the ball, then Martin took two quick steps forward and curled the ball over the wall with his left foot. The connection felt good as the ball left his foot, and he watched it float towards the top corner. It dipped at the perfect moment and he saw the net ripple.

Gooooooooooooooooooooaaaaaaaaaaaaaaaaalllllllllllllll llllllllllll!!!!!!!!!!!!!!!!!!!

Martin ran over towards the touchline, patting the Arsenal badge on his shirt and jumping in the air.

'You couldn't have hit that any better!' Thomas shouted, wrapping him in a hug.

Even though Martin wasn't much older than some of his teammates, he had been through a lot in his career and the younger players were soon coming to him with questions and looking for advice.

Arsenal went into the last two months of the 2021–22 season with a real chance of qualifying for the Champions League, but then the wobbles came back. They were outplayed in a 3–0 loss to Crystal Palace, then went 2–0 down at home to Brighton before a frantic finish. Desperate times called for desperate shots – and Martin's long-range shot looped off a Brighton defender and flew into the top corner.

Goooooooooooooooooooooaaaaaaaaaaaaaaaaalllllllllllllll llllllllllll!!!!!!!!!!!!!!!!!!!

The Arsenal players ran to get the ball, but it was too little, too late. A loss to Southampton in their next game set off more alarm bells.

But Martin had been through enough battles to know that Arsenal could get back on track quickly. Away to Chelsea, he was everywhere. At 1–1, he swept the ball wide to Bukayo and carried on his run to the edge of the box. Bukayo laid the ball back to him, and Martin saw Emile Smith Rowe charging forward to his left. With a pass that was just right – not too strong, not too weak – Martin set up Emile to place the ball in the bottom corner.

Yes! Martin pounded the grass with both hands in celebration and ran over to join his teammates. Though Chelsea equalised again, Arsenal held their nerve and hit back again for a 4–2 win. The relief was clear as the players celebrated with the small section of fans at the end of the game, and they won their next three league games too.

But the race for a Champions League spot was always likely to come down to a North London derby against Tottenham. It was Arsenal's biggest game of the season – and it seemed as if they barely showed up. Tottenham won 3–0 and Martin couldn't believe that they were throwing away all the hard work. A 2–0 loss away to Newcastle in their next game was almost as bad.

Martin scored the fifth goal in a 5–1 victory against

Everton, on the last day of the season, but it was all out of Arsenal's hands by that point. Tottenham clinched fourth place and a long, painful summer began. It was a horrible feeling.

The next few days were tough, and Martin didn't want to see anyone or speak to anyone while he got over the shock of missing out on a return to the Champions League. But eventually he dragged himself back to the training ground to see some of his teammates and coaches before they all headed off for different holidays. It helped Martin to see some familiar faces, and Mikel was already looking ahead and focusing on the positives.

'I'm already excited about what we can achieve next season – and you're a big reason for that,' Mikel said as he and Martin sat down in the Arsenal cafeteria just before the summer break. 'You were back to your best this year – and this team has a very bright future.'

CHAPTER 21

HANGING OUT WITH HAALAND

These days, Martin wasn't the only young Norway star who was being talked about. Erling Haaland had become an unstoppable goal machine for Borussia Dortmund in the German league. As they spent more time together with the national team squad, a strong friendship developed between them. Sometimes they talked about how they could have been teammates at Dortmund, had Martin decided differently all those years ago when he left Strømsgodset.

In many ways, they were total opposites, and their personalities were very different. Martin was quieter, Erling was louder. On the pitch, they didn't have a lot in common either. Martin was more about skill and movement, and Erling was all pace and power. But they were instantly connected by having lived with the same pressure and expectations from a young age.

Almost every player had to deal with challenges on the way to becoming a professional, but Martin and Erling had faced a whole different level of attention. Often, it was just nice to speak to someone else who really understood the ups and downs of the journey. Neither of them had lived a normal life as teenagers.

'People don't always realise what it's like to have that "next big thing" tag,' Martin said as they caught up before the latest Norway game. 'But you really can't predict anything in football. Look at the path I took – Real Madrid, three loans and finally Arsenal. Through a lot of that, I was still just a kid.'

Erling nodded. 'The last few years have been great, but all the hype started while I was still learning the game and playing against older boys every week. It definitely made me grow up faster, because you have to when there's that much attention on you.'

But that was all behind them now, and their shared goal was to put Norway back in contention for the major tournaments. Feeding off their friendship, they had developed a great connection on the pitch too. Erling loved to get behind defences, and Martin was so good at sliding passes through to him before defenders could react.

'We've got a great opportunity now with Norway,' Martin said. 'I really like the team we're building around the two of us, and we can grow together as a group over the next ten years.'

Erling was never short of confidence. 'We can beat anyone on our day,' he replied. 'World Cup, Euros, whatever – bring it on!'

'Well, let's just focus on getting into one of those tournaments first,' Martin said, laughing. 'We'll be instant heroes if we qualify.'

Martin had enjoyed telling Erling stories about his time at Arsenal, and his friend had definitely been asking more questions about life in England lately.

'Are you still liking the Premier League?' Erling asked, as they took a quick break from the latest training session.

Martin thought for a few seconds. 'Joining Arsenal is one of the best decisions I've ever made,' he said. 'The Premier League is great. I love the end-to-end action and I feel like I'm playing the best football of my life there.'

'Very cool,' Erling continued. 'I like watching the games on TV and it always seems like a faster pace than other leagues in Europe.'

'Yeah, that took me by surprise at first, but it's physical, it's fast and, well... you'd love it,' Martin explained.

'Well, I might be seeing all of that for myself soon,' Erling added, with a cheeky smile and a shrug. 'There are lots of reports about Manchester City wanting to sign me.'

Martin felt like telling Erling that London was the place to be, but he didn't want to mess with his friend's decision. It would be fun to have his friend living in the same country, even if he was playing for a different team.

Sure enough, later that summer, Martin's phone buzzed with a four-word message from Erling: 'I'm joining Man City.'

Wow. That was big news – and it was going to shake up the Premier League too. Martin knew better than most that Erling was a defender's nightmare.

'Can we still be friends?' Martin joked back.

But any club rivalries would be set aside when it was time to play for Norway, and Martin couldn't wait to see what he and Erling would achieve together.

CHAPTER 22

LEADING THE PREMIER LEAGUE TITLE CHARGE

Martin loved all the sounds and smells of preseason – the freshly cut pitches, the last of the summer sunshine in England and all the exciting possibilities before the action kicked off. He was even more excited for the 2022–23 season when Mikel named him as the new Arsenal captain.

Pierre-Emerick had left midway through last season and Mikel had chosen to rotate the captain's armband at that stage rather than appoint an official replacement. But now it was time for a fresh start, and Mikel decided that Martin was the right man to lead this young Arsenal team.

'Over the past eighteen months since he joined us,' Mikel told reporters, 'he's represented the values of this football club, the team, the teammates and the staff in the best possible way. He's displayed an ambition to take this club to a different level, to push this team and contribute within it, and he is respected by everyone inside the organisation.'

The only thing missing in Martin's time in London was a trophy, and he put that right during the preseason as Arsenal won the Emirates Cup. But the biggest competitions lay ahead – and Arsenal needed to prove that they had learned from last season's setbacks. Mikel had been busy over the summer, bringing in Gabriel Jesus and Oleksandr Zinchenko from Manchester City to add quality and experience to the dressing room.

Big speeches weren't really Martin's thing, but when he did speak up, people listened. He told his teammates how much he believed in them and how excited he was for them to chase trophies together.

Martin also pointed to the season's predictions that were already appearing – Arsenal were not a popular pick to finish in the top three.

'But why not us?' Martin asked, looking around the

dressing room. His teammates cheered and clapped.

Arsenal made a promising start, winning their first two games, and Martin loved seeing all the scoring chances they were creating. Standing at the front of the line in the tunnel ready to face Bournemouth, he was already picturing scoring that afternoon. He had been making so many good runs into the box, but he was still looking for his first goal of the season. He wouldn't have to wait much longer.

After just five minutes, Gabriel Jesus set up Gabriel Martinelli and his shot rebounded straight to Martin. Martin didn't even have to move. He just poked the ball into the net with his left foot.

Goooooooooooooooooooooaaaaaaaaaaaaaaaaaalllllllllllllllll llllllllllll!!!!!!!!!!!!!!!!!!!

It was as easy a goal as he would ever score, but Martin didn't care. He jogged over to celebrate with the travelling Arsenal fans.

He was soon back over there again. Bukayo got the Bournemouth defenders backpedalling, Jesus controlled the cross and Martin pounced on the loose ball, smashing in a quick shot before anyone could react.

Gooooooooooooooooooooaaaaaaaaaaaaaaaalllllllllllllll llllllllllll!!!!!!!!!!!!!!!!!!!!

Arsenal were on their way to five wins out of five in August – and that was exactly the message that Martin wanted to send to the other title contenders.

One of the common criticisms during Martin's career, especially in his stops at Castilla and Heerenveen, was a lack of goals. But he was silencing all of that this season. He scored to spark a comeback against Fulham, then netted again at home to Nottingham Forest.

'We're already surprising people this year,' Martin told his parents proudly. 'No one was picking us to be a contender, but this team is capable of doing something really special.'

There was no time for complacency with recent results, Martin stressed, because new games and new challenges were always there. He made that point repeatedly during the warm-up away to Wolves, sensing it was the kind of game where Arsenal had slipped up in the past. It was the last Premier League game before the 2022 World Cup and Martin was determined to go into the midseason break on a high note.

After a goalless first half, Mikel urged his team to keep attacking, and Martin still felt full of energy to make his midfield runs. It would only take one magic moment to unlock this Wolves defence. Fábio Vieira got free on the left and Martin raced into the box. He saw the angle for a cutback was too tight – so he ran on, hoping for a ball fizzed low near the keeper. That's exactly what Fábio provided, and Martin got there first for a tap-in, just in front of Bukayo. *1–0!*

Gooooooooooooooooooooaaaaaaaaaaaaaaaaalllllllllllllll llllllllllll!!!!!!!!!!!!!!!!!!!!!

He grabbed the Arsenal badge on his shirt as Bukayo jumped on his back. 'You little thief!' Bukayo joked. 'You took that goal right off my foot.'

Now Arsenal were racing forward and everyone wanted a touch of the ball. Next, it was Oleksandr's turn to find space on the left, and his cross bounced around in the box before looping towards Martin. Even in a crowded penalty area, Martin knew he had time to control the ball, so he cushioned it with the inside of his left boot and then thumped a shot past the lunging defenders and the diving keeper.

Goooooooooooooooooooooaaaaaaaaaaaaaaaaalllllllllllllll llllllllllllll!!!!!!!!!!!!!!!!!!!!

While Bukayo, Gabriel Jesus, Granit and so many other internationals caught their flights for the World Cup, Martin was left with a month of free time. But he wasn't going to sulk about Norway not being at the tournament. Instead, he focused on resting and being as fresh as possible when the season restarted at the end of December.

That plan worked well: Martin scored key goals in December and January to keep Arsenal top of the table, including a memorable two-goal game against Tottenham. Erling and Manchester City were looking like the biggest threat, creeping closer with a win over the Gunners in February.

But, just like the previous season, April was a nightmare month for Arsenal. They stumbled to three draws in a row, then they were blown away by City in a heartbreaking 4–1 loss. Martin and his teammates had rescued themselves from some tight spots during the season, but that magic had worn off just when Arsenal needed to be at their best.

Martin hoped there would be plenty more battles for the Premier League title, but this time it was Erling and City who swooped in to lift the trophy. Arsenal had spent so much of the season in first place, and they had been playing so well that he had allowed himself to picture what it would be like to be champions of England.

Martin tried to push all those thoughts from his mind ahead of his summer break. There was nothing he could do about it now, except use the disappointment as a spark for next season.

'We're going to come back even stronger,' Martin explained when he joined his family for lunch. 'It's nice to be here with you and have some time off, and then I'll be counting the days until I'm back chasing trophies again!'

Turn the page for a sneak preview of another brilliant football story by Matt and Tom Oldfield. . . SAKA!

CHAPTER 1

ENGLAND'S NEW EURO 2020 HERO

22 June 2021, Wembley Stadium

As Harry Kane led the England team out onto the pitch, there was a crowd of nearly 20,000 excited fans waiting for them. After two years of playing in empty stadiums due to the COVID-19 pandemic, the roar sounded so good.

Come on England, come on England!

Most of the line-up had already experienced the electric Wembley atmosphere after featuring in their first two matches at Euro 2020 – a 1–0 win over Croatia, followed by a disappointing 0–0 draw with Scotland. But for their final must-win group game against the Czech Republic, the England manager Gareth Southgate had made some changes in attack. Jack Grealish for Mason Mount was a swap that most people were expecting, but the replacement of Phil Foden on the right wing was much more of a surprise. Not with Marcus Rashford, or Jadon Sancho, but with Bukayo Saka!

At the age of only nineteen, Arsenal's rising star was about to represent England in a major tournament! Just being named in England's Euro 2020 squad had been a lovely surprise, but to be selected in the starting line-up – it was beyond Bukayo's wildest dreams.

As he stood and sang the national anthem, though, Bukayo didn't look nervous or worried at all. Why should he have been, though? He had worked so hard for this opportunity, ever since signing for Arsenal at the age of seven. At the Euros, he had been watching, waiting and learning as much as possible from the senior England players every day in training. He had successfully impressed Southgate with his talent and attitude, and now, it was time to give his all on the pitch for his country.

'Let's win this!' Kyle Walker cheered as the anthem ended. With all his experience, he was the perfect player for Bukayo to have behind him on the right side for England. Although he often played on the left for Arsenal, either in defence or midfield, Bukayo had the speed, skill, intelligence and energy to play in almost any position. That's why his managers loved him so much – he was such a useful footballer to have around.

As well as his work-rate, there was one other reason why Bukayo was the right man for the job: he had humiliated the Czech left-back, Jan Bořil, once before in the Europa League quarter-final. That night, Arsenal's young winger had grabbed a goal and an assist, while the Slavia Prague defender was taken off at half-time.

So, could Bukayo embarrass Bořil again? He was involved in the game almost straight away, as he calmly chested the ball down and played a simple pass back to Kyle. It was a good start, but now he needed to push forward and attack.

'Just do what you do at Arsenal,' Southgate had told him in the dressing room. 'Play with confidence and freedom, and enjoy yourself.'

Yes, Boss! In the eleventh minute, Bukayo dropped deep to collect the ball off Kyle, and then spun and dribbled forward at speed, leaving the Czech midfielders trailing behind him. After crossing the halfway line, he passed the ball to Kalvin Phillips, but Bukayo didn't stop there. No, he kept on running into the box for the one-two.

When the return pass arrived, Bukayo twisted and turned away from two defenders and delivered a deep cross to the back post, but it was too high for Harry. Eventually, it came out to Jack on the left wing, who curled in another cross. As the ball floated across the six-yard box, Bukayo made his move, from the right to the middle. He leapt up high to meet it, but unfortunately, it flew just over his head. But there was no need to worry; Raheem Sterling was right behind him and he nodded the ball into the net. *1–0!* Hurray, England were winning at Wembley!

'Come on!' Bukayo cried out, punching the air with passion. With the fans cheering wildly, he rushed over to celebrate with his teammates. He hadn't scored the goal himself, but he had played an important part in setting it up. On his way back for the restart, he stopped to remove his underlayer. It was too hot to wear two shirts; he was on fire!

England had the goal they needed, but Bukayo wanted more. Every time he got the ball, his first thought was, 'Attack!' And so he dribbled forward again and again, forcing Bořil to back away in fear. Although he couldn't quite find the killer final pass to Harry or Raheem, Bukayo was causing all kinds of problems for the Czech defence.

'Unlucky, keep going!' Southgate clapped and cheered on the sidelines.

Yes, Boss! Bukayo showed more of the same fearlessness in the second half. As he received the ball with his back to goal, he had a Czech player right behind him, but he used his strength to hold him off and then chipped a brilliant pass through to Harry.

'What a ball!' the England fans roared. Bukayo was fast becoming one of their favourite players.

As the game went on, Bořil grew more and more frustrated by his impressive opponent. Every time he tried to close him down, Bukayo somehow managed to wriggle away until eventually, the defender tripped him up and dragged him to the floor. Yellow card! Oh dear, Bořil was having another bad day against Bukayo.

For all his attacking flair, Bukayo was also happy to chase back and do his defensive duties when needed. As a left-back at Arsenal, he had learned to track his marker and be in the right position to make the block.

'Nice one, mate!' Kyle shouted as he cleared the ball away upfield.

After eighty-four amazing minutes, Bukayo's dream Euro 2020 debut came to an end. As he walked off, all the England fans rose to their feet to clap for their new national hero.

'Well played, bro,' said Marcus and Jadon, giving him high-fives as he left the field.

'Wow, what a performance!' said Southgate on the touchline, giving him a great big hug.

At last, Bukayo allowed his focus to drop and a smile to spread across his face. Yes, he had certainly made the most of his chance to shine at Euro 2020.

England held on to win 1–0 and finish top of

Group D. Next up, in the Round of 16, they would face their old enemies Germany, but that could wait. For now, all everyone was talking about was the man of the match: Bukayo! The boy from Ealing, West London, had just burst onto the scene as England's new superstar. What an exciting future he had ahead of him.

CHAPTER 2

EARLY KICKS IN EALING

'Where is he? He's LATE!'

While they waited impatiently for their father to get home from work, Bukayo and his older brother Yomi did the only thing they could do: they practised inside, kicking a balloon up in the air between them. It just wasn't the same, though. Nothing compared to the real thing, and that's why they needed their father to hurry up and get home – so that they could go outside and play a proper game with him!

Yomi Senior had fallen in love with football long before he moved to England from Nigeria, but with the chance to watch the Premier League on TV every week, his passion for the sport had grown stronger and stronger. Although the Sakas lived in Ealing, West London, he didn't support Chelsea, or Tottenham, or Arsenal. No, instead he supported Newcastle United. Why them? Because his favourite player was their striker, Alan Shearer. By 2005, Shearer's career was coming to an end, 'but you should have seen him when he was younger,' he often told his boys. 'What a superstar he was!'

There was one thing, though, that Yomi Senior loved even more than watching and talking about football, and that was playing it. And being able to play the beautiful game with his sons was exactly that – beautiful. He enjoyed every minute of it, after work and especially at the weekends.

'Quick, he's coming!' Yomi Jr called out suddenly.

Together, the brothers watched through the window with great excitement as at last their father approached their house. As soon as he was through the front door, he dropped his work bag and hugged his sons.

'Sorry boys, Shearer's back! Right, are you ready for a quick game?'

'Yayyyyyy!'

Grabbing the ball from the cupboard, Yomi Sr led his sons outside and onto the pitch. In reality, their garden was just a small square of grass, but through the young boys' eyes, it was as wonderful and important as any big football stadium.

'Okay, you're the youngest Bukayo, so you can start with the ball today,' their dad decided.

Yes, Yomi Jr was older, but his competitive younger brother was catching up quickly. Each and every day, Bukayo's left foot was growing more powerful and his football skills were improving: his ball control, passing, dribbling, shooting. He was determined to become the best footballer in the family as soon as possible.

Bukayo's name meant 'adds to happiness' in Yoruba, one of Nigeria's main languages, and most of the time, he was a very happy four-year-old boy. If he was losing on the family football pitch, however, his smile soon disappeared.

'Can we go inside now? I'm hungry!' Yomi Jr complained after a while.

Bukayo shook his head and clenched his fists. It was

easy for his brother to say that; he was winning. 'No, we haven't finished the game yet.'

'Come on, son, your brother's right. It's getting dark – we can carry on tomorrow.'

'No!'

Sometimes, the two Yomis managed to persuade him to stop, but usually, they agreed to play on until Bukayo was the winner. It was easier for everyone that way.

'Cool, can we go inside and eat now?' his brother asked.

'Yesssssssss!' he replied, with a big smile back on his face.

For Bukayo, those garden games were just the beginning. Once he got a bit older, he was allowed to go out and play on his own on the green in front of their house. Much better; now he had more space and there was no-one there to stop him. Most nights, he would be out there for hours, practising the same ball skills again and again until bedtime.

'He's certainly got the dedication to be a professional player one day,' Yomi said to his wife,

Adenike, as they watched their hard-working son through the window.

Yes, but what about the talent? The Sakas would have to wait and see, but the next step was finding Bukayo a first football team.

SAKA

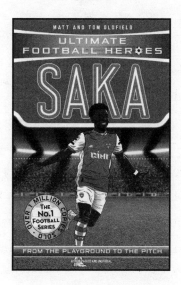

Available now!

ØDEGAARD
HONOURS

Real Sociedad

🏆 Copa del Rey: 2019–20

Individual

🏆 Norwegian League Young Player of the Year: 2014

🏆 Eredivisie Team of the Year: 2018–19

🏆 Vitesse Player of the Year: 2018–19

🏆 Gullballen (Norwegian Footballer of the Year): 2019

🏆 La Liga Player of the Month: September 2019

🏆 Premier League Player of the Month: November/ December 2022

🏆 London Football Awards Premier League Player of the Year: 2023

GREATEST MOMENTS

16 MAY 2014,
STRØMSGODSET 4–1 SARPSBORG

Many people in Norway already knew about 'Young Messi', but in this match, Martin made a name for himself around the world. He came on in the seventieth minute to make his professional league debut, aged just fifteen, and by the time the final whistle blew, he had already scored his first senior goal! A new superstar had just burst onto the scene.

10 NOVEMBER 2018,
VITESSE 2–1 UTRECHT

After a slow start at Real Madrid and then a frustrating first loan at Heerenveen, Martin really came alive at Vitesse. In this league match, he capped off a star performance by fizzing a curling free kick over the wall and into the net. The goalkeeper didn't even stand a chance of saving it.

6 FEBRUARY 2020,
REAL MADRID 3–4 REAL SOCIEDAD

Martin enjoyed another excellent loan spell at Spanish team Real Sociedad and in this quarter-final Copa del Rey clash, he really showed his main club what they were missing. In the twenty-second minute, he fired in a low shot that nutmegged a Real Madrid defender and the keeper. Thanks to Martin's magic, Sociedad went on to win the match and the Spanish Cup.

14 MARCH 2021, ARSENAL 2–1 TOTTENHAM

This definitely wasn't one of the best goals that Martin has ever scored, but it was a very important one. With his loan club losing 1–0 in the North London derby, Martin scuffed a shot that somehow confused the Tottenham keeper and trickled into the corner. The Gunners went on to win 2–1 and soon Martin was a permanent Arsenal player.

15 JANUARY 2023, TOTTENHAM 0–2 ARSENAL

Although in the end, Arsenal couldn't quite hold on to top spot and lift the Premier League title, they had a fantastic 2022–23 season. This North London derby was a very special victory for the Gunners and Martin was their match-winning hero yet again. In the thirty-sixth minute, his low, hard, left-foot shot skidded off the pitch and arrowed into the bottom corner.

PLAY LIKE YOUR HEROES

HIT CURLING FREE KICKS
LIKE MARTIN ØDEGAARD

Step 1: As an attacking midfielder, it's your job to create goalscoring chances for your team with your skill and vision. Keep making clever runs into space, and then once you get the ball, dribble forward with it until you spot a defence-splitting pass, or... *FOUL – FREE KICK!*

Step 2: Here we go – your big opportunity. It's fine for other teammates to stand around the ball too, but make it clear that you want to take the free kick. You're feeling confident – this one is yours.

Step 3: While you wait for the referee's whistle, look up and study the situation carefully. Is there a tall wall in front of you, or can you see a smart way around it? Is the keeper standing in the middle of the goal, or over to one side? Then, when the whistle blows, look down at the ball and get ready...

Step 4: If the keeper is standing in the middle, then you've got to make sure your free kick is unstoppable. Take a few quick steps towards the ball and then – *BANG!* – curl it with plenty of power towards the top-corner.

Step 5: If the keeper is standing a long way to the left, it's time for a surprise. Run up as if you're going to curl it top left like usual, but at the last second, swivel your body and whip the ball up over the wall and then dip it down into the bottom right corner instead .

Step 6: Either way, what a free kick – *GOAL!* Jump up and punch the air, slide towards the corner flag on your knees, kiss the badge on your shirt – whatever you do, enjoy the magical moment.

TEST YOUR KNOWLEDGE

QUESTIONS

1. What position did Martin's dad, Hans Erik, play on the football pitch?

2. How did Martin first become an Arsenal fan?

3. What position did Martin play first for the Elite Academy Under 13s?

4. Which of Martin's football heroes did his Strømsgodset teammates compare him to?

5. How old was Martin when he made his first-team debut for Strømsgodset?

6. Martin became the youngest player ever to play in a European Championship qualifier. What country was he playing against?

7. Which French football legend helped persuade Martin to sign for Real Madrid?

8. Which two Dutch clubs did Martin play for on loan?

9. True or false – Martin beat Real Madrid while playing for a different club?

10. Who did Martin replace as Arsenal captain?

11. Which friend and international teammate joined Martin in the Premier League for the 2022–23 season?

*1. He was a midfielder. 2. Through playing FIFA! 3. Left-back.
4. Lionel Messi. 5. Only fifteen! 6. Bulgaria. 7. Zinedine Zidane.
8. Heerenveen and Vitesse .9. True! He helped Real Sociedad to win their
Copa del Rey quarter-final clash. 10. Pierre-Emerick Aubameyang.
11. Erling Haaland.*

ØDEGAARD

8

THE FACTS

NAME: Martin Ødegaard

DATE OF BIRTH: 17 December 1998

PLACE OF BIRTH: Drammen

NATIONALITY: Norway

BEST FRIENDS: Erling Haaland

CURRENT CLUB: Arsenal

POSITION: CAM

THE STATS

Height (cm):	178
Club appearances:	331
Club goals:	57
Club assists:	0
Club trophies:	1
International appearances:	49
International goals:	2
International trophies:	0
Ballon d'Ors:	0

★ ★ ★ **HERO RATING: 87** ★ ★ ★

CAN'T GET ENOUGH OF
ULTIMATE FOOTBALL HEROES?

Check out heroesfootball.com
for quizzes, games, and competitions!

Plus join the Ultimate Football Heroes
Fan Club to score exclusive content and
be the first to hear about
new books and events.
heroesfootball.com/subscribe/